COSMOPOLITAN
Vegetarian
Cookbook

Also published by Robson Books

Cosmopolitan Meals in Minutes
Cosmopolitan Perfect Pasta

COSMOPOLITAN
Vegetarian
Cookbook

Amanda Grant

Robson Books

First published in Great Britain in 1998 by Robson Books Ltd, Bolsover House, 5–6 Clipstone Street, London W1P 8LE

British Library Cataloguing in Publication Data
A catalogue record for this title is available from the British Library

ISBN 1 86105 203 0

Typeset by Textype Typesetters, Cambridge
Printed by WBC Book Manufacturers, Bridgend

For David, Pop and the boys

Acknowledgements

First of all my very special thanks go to David, my husband, for his support, encouragement and above all, for being the most dedicated taster I know. His constructive comments are always welcome.

I would also like to thank Carol Bronze, my Managing Editor at Cosmopolitan, who has a fabulous enthusiasm for food and is a delight to work with. It was always a goal of mine to write for the number one woman's magazine and it is a great joy to have written a book, too. On that note, I would like to thank Emma Dally, for asking me to write the *Vegetarian Cookbook* and for her support and encouragement throughout.

Thanks, too, to Kate Mills and Anthea Matthison at Robson Books for their attention to detail and excitement about the recipes. There are many other writers, chefs, delis, PR companies and supermarkets whom I would also love to thank for their tips, recipe ideas, new ingredients, advice and time.

Contents

Starters

Soups

Almost Instant

15 Minutes or Longer

Puddings and Sauces

Sauces

Introduction

I love and believe passionately in vegetarian food which I eat in vast quantities, although not exclusively. Let's get one thing straight, the *Cosmopolitan Vegetarian Cookbook* is not about cooking lots of lentils or nut roasts, it is about enjoying lots of our favourite ingredients, like pasta, rice, vegetables, fruit and nuts, in an inspirational and quick way. It is an exciting topic for a *Cosmopolitan* cookbook as it is a chance to share recipes that really are fresh, fast and fashionable. This is a cookbook for vegetarians and non-vegetarians alike, to dip in and out of.

I have highlighted the recipes in the book suitable for vegans with a V; the difference being; vegetarians do not eat meat, poultry or fish; vegans do not eat any food that is a derivative of animals, that is dairy food or byproducts derived from animals like gelatine.

Fashionable

There are so many fabulous, often foreign, vegetarian ingredients available in the shops today, including the local supermarket, that it makes it easy to develop imaginative vegetarian recipes that can be cooked at home. In other words, we eat out and taste these amazing dishes that have a real foreign flavour but we can now have a go at similar, but often much easier, dishes at home.

I have taken a selection of the more unusual, with everyday ingredients, added a little imagination and a short amount of time to create a range of quick and modern vegetarian recipes for you to have fun cooking and enjoy eating. Well, I certainly enjoyed developing them and judging by the size of my chief tasters who consumed two or three dishes each night, they also enjoyed eating them.

Some of the recipes have been influenced by the flavours from Japan, others Morocco. Many of the recipes have a Mediterranean flavour, inspired by holidays and time spent in Italy, France and Spain.

Recipes for Everyone

The most important thing to remember is that these recipes are for everyone, vegetarians and ardent carnivores – the latter may like to get their teeth into some of these dishes every now and then as well as occasionally eating fish or chicken alongside.

Fast

We are busy, there is no denying it, and often we choose what to eat depending on how long we will have to spend in the kitchen or how long it will take in the oven. So, to help you make that decision, I have broken the recipes down to those that really are quick, those that require about 15 minutes (depending on how long it takes you to chop an onion) and those that need more than 30 minutes – giving you the chance to do something else while it cooks in the oven.

Flexible

Many of the recipes are suitable and scrummy for a variety of occasions – whether for a simple supper at home or a dinner party for a few friends. I hope to show you that you do not need to spend a long time making fancy or elaborate dishes to impress. It is possible, when entertaining, to spend a minimum time in the kitchen and a lot of time with the guests.

Easy

I believe the recipes in this book are straightforward and easy to follow. I have given quantities where I feel it is necessary but, in some recipes, where personal taste is more important than an exact gram or ounce, I have left measurements more flexible.

Vegetarian Diet and Nutrition

A vegetarian diet, with or without dairy food, can supply all the nutrients needed for health and vitality. There is more and more evidence that a vegetarian diet of fresh, natural and, where possible, raw foods, not processed and not refined, can help reduce the incidence of cancer, heart disease, diabetes and other afflictions.

There is no need to panic about eating the correct balance of vegetarian food, all we need to do is eat a good *mix* of ingredients. To help us understand what a good mix should include, here are a few sources of each of the essential nutrients.

Vitamins and Minerals

There are so many fresh foods that contain vitamins and minerals, but the main source is fresh raw fruit and vegetables.

B vitamins can be found in almonds, cashews, pecans, pine nuts, also in dried apricots and our friend Marmite.

The only vitamin that is found naturally in animal products is vitamin B12. This is not a problem for vegetarians who eat dairy food and eggs, Vegans, however, need to eat foods that have been fortified with the vitamin, e.g. soya milk, yeast extract and breakfast cereals.

Vitamin D is found in dairy products, fortified foods like cereals (always check the label) and soya milk.

The mineral iron is often a cause of concern for vegetarians. A diet deficient in this mineral can lead to anaemia, tiredness and a general rundown feeling. Good sources of iron include pumpkin and sesame seeds; once again, lots of nuts (cashew, walnuts, hazelnuts, brazil, pecans and peanuts); beans, dried figs, raisins, chickpeas, red kidney beans and Popeye's spinach.

It is a good idea to eat vitamin C rich foods at the same time as iron rich foods as this helps to ensure that the iron present is utilized to its full. For example, pour fruit juice (a good source of vitamin C) on a nutty muesli (good source of iron) instead of milk.

The only other mineral I would quite like to mention is calcium because it often suprises people to learn that, aside from dairy products, calcium is found in leafy green vegetables (e.g. bok choi, kale), broccoli, figs, sesame seeds, almonds (yet again), soya milk, tahini (paste made from sesame seeds) and molasses.

Carbohydrate (including sugars and starches)

Carbohydrate is the body's main source of energy. Good sources include breads, cereals, pastas, potatoes, fruit and vegetables. Refined sugars and lots of sugary snacks are foods to avoid.

Fat

Most obvious sources include oils, seeds, nuts, grains and dairy products. However, you can consume enough fat from the first four more valuable sources without needing to eat too many dairy products.

Protein

Protein deficiency in vegetarians or vegans is virtually impossible providing sufficient calories are eaten. There are so many foods that contain protein: eggs, dairy and soya products, brown rice, wholegrains, peas, seeds, nuts, beans, some vegetables and lentils.

Contrary to belief, it is not necessary to eat dairy food for protein. Plant sources alone can be sufficient, if a variety is consumed. For example, eat a mixture of nuts and seeds for a snack or tossed over salads; for lunch have a bean dish with fresh bread, e.g., Cannellini beans and olives with fresh Italian bread or a chickpea dip with toasted pitta; at supper eat a rice dish with a handful of nuts scattered over the top, e.g., green rice with soy nuts.

Stocking the Cupboard

The key to successful and smart cooking is not to have lots in the cupboard, just the essentials . . .

Essentials

Most of the following ingredients are available in large supermarkets; for those that are not, I have recommended places where you might look. I am not suggesting that you need to buy all of these ingredients straight away, but this section is a good guide as to the sort of thing you may find it useful to keep in the cupboard.

You often only need a few ingredients to rustle up a supper but the skill lies in coming up with the combination. If you can at least turn to a cupboard containing some of these essentials, life does become a whole lot easier (yes, I was once a Girl Guide).

Grains: couscous, polenta, bulgar wheat, porridge oats. My current passion is for couscous (tiny little grains of semolina coated in wheat flour) because it is so quick and easy to use. As for polenta, it does require a little more effort, but it is worth it. The other thing to note is that often only a couple of ingredients are needed – a bowl of polenta with butter and parmesan is comfort food from heaven.

Rice: basmati, Thai and arborio (or other risotto rice). Thanks to food writer Roz Denny, I adore basmati. She showed me how to ensure success every time I cook it and it always tastes delicious. Another favourite is Thai rice, which has its own wonderful flavour. Arborio is always good to have on standby (promise me you will never cook a risotto with anything other than a true risotto rice).

Pasta: choose a few favourites. A large flat one like pappardelle is always good to have; short, curly macaroni; tagliatelle; egg noodles and rice noodles (which are so quick) would make a sensible set.

Nuts and seeds: pumpkin and sunflower seeds are both easy to use (see the Nibbles section) and a handful of nuts (especially almonds, cashew or brazil) toasted and tossed in olive oil, is always a quick treat.

Tinned beans and pulses: chickpeas, cannellini beans, kidney beans, butter beans, puy lentils and green lentils are my favourite. They require no soaking or precooking, but give them a good rinse under the tap before using them to wash off the sugar or salt often found in their water.

Sauces: chutneys, mustards (wholegrain), olive pastes, pesto, harissa, dark and light soy sauces, passatta – it is always a good idea to keep a few of these in the cupboard, a little chutney and brown butter and you have a sauce in an instant. Harissa is great tossed over couscous. Soy sauces pep up stir fries and pasta tossed in an olive paste with a little olive oil and parmesan is often all you need at the end of a long day.

Tins: there are only a couple of ingredients that work really well in tins, aside from our beans and pulses, namely coconut milk, sweetcorn, and tomatoes (Cirio from Italy are the best brand). For quick sweet snack attacks, a tin of creamed rice pudding (with lashings of syrup) does the trick.

Oils: if you have space for several types, go for a light olive oil and an extra virgin. My favourite has got to be Carapelli extra virgin oil from Italy. The latter is great for salad dressings and drizzling over lightly cooked vegetables or finished dishes (although I must confess, I do tend to use extra virgin for everything, I just love it). Go for a bland groundnut oil, as well for frying. Another favourite for salad dressings is the faithful walnut oil; just mix with a little lemon or lime juice. If you are looking for a fourth oil, I would go for sesame. I do not tend to use this one often, but it is in a recipe that the head chef from the Table Café at Habitat gave to me, so I feel it should be mentioned.

Vinegars: balsamic is the one essential vinegar that requires spending a little bit of cash on to get a good dark, sweet and rich, yet mellow flavour. Rice wine vinegar is also an essential. I remember when it required time and patience to find this little ingredient, now all you need to do is pop into the nearest supermarket. Cider vinegar and red wine are also worth keeping, but have a look at the sauces later in the book and you may prefer to make one or two dressings and keep to those vinegars rather than storing all four.

Spices: my advice is to keep a few whole spices like green cardamom pods, coriander seeds, black peppercorns, cinnamon sticks, nutmeg and dried chillies (see page 21) and grind them as and when required. Another spice worth keeping is star anise (see Berry Soup on page 183, for a recipe idea that uses it to its full). Not forgetting our pretty and useful friend saffron. Vanilla pods are nice to have for those quick custards, or scrape out the seeds and mix into crème fraiche.
Quick tip: add dried orange or lime zest to your peppermill for a wonderful fresh seasoning.

Sea salt flakes (Maldon): have such a wonderfully strong taste of the sea that you will find yourself using less than normal salt.

Jams: with a high fruit content and little sugar and a good runny honey.

Unrefined sugars: are the only sugars to use. A spoonful of muscovado sugar or golden icing sugar mixed with yogurt (see page 178) can only be described as gooey fudge on a spoon. I will never make any puddings, biscuits, cakes or meringues without this essential ingredient ever again. Look out for Billington's or own label sugars but check on the label that it says unrefined, otherwise you may be buying a white sugar that has been coloured brown.

Recommended Luxuries

I felt that I was being too indulgent to include the following under the heading Essentials, but they are too important not to mention at all.

Kaffir lime leaves: there is something almost magical about these leaves – they do not have the same strong citric flavour as the juice from the fruit but are more aromatic. Experiment with them: add them into the water when you are cooking rice or pasta.

Pickled ginger: the wonderful Japanese ingredient that adds a kick to food in the most convenient and pleasing form. Watch out for the bright pink kind – the colour indicates the presence of a nasty dye.

Wasabi: it may look like toothpaste in a squeezy tube, but don't be fooled. Squeeze it into a little pot and use with caution – it's Japanese horseradish with a real attitude.

Finally, a few bottles of white and red wine are a good store-cupboard ingredient and a couple of liqueurs for those fruit desserts.

Stocking the Fridge

Cheese: a couple of good versatile cheeses. (Experiment with different ones: Parmesan, ricotta, Cheddar, Gorgonzola, Gruyère, mascarpone, Mozzarella, fontina, goat's cheese). Also crème fraiche, Stilton, Brie, Camembert, dolcelatte.

Crème fraiche and yogurt: are always useful ingredients. They can thin out sauces, provide a base for a dip or a dreamy dessert swirled with a good quality jam.

A tube of fresh croissant dough: you can twist and bake the dough as it is for a quick and impressive breakfast or add a few other ingredients for a supper dish.

Leafy green vegetables: a packet of spinach or watercress.

Fresh herbs: if you can keep growing herbs, do. A handful of fresh herbs adds aroma, colour and flavour to a dish that cannot be achieved so simply and effectively by any other ingredient.

Fresh ginger: a knobbly root keeps for a long time if wrapped in kitchen paper and kept in a bag.

Chillies: as a general guide, skinny and thin chillies are hotter than those with broad shoulders, although the Scotch Bonnet chilli proves otherwise. So make sure you taste the food as you are making it, add a little – you can always add more. As soon as you add coconut milk, or any other high-fat liquid, to chilli or chilli paste, the taste will become milder. Another interesting fact about chillies is that fresh chillies with wrinkled skins are hotter than the smooth kind. But if dried chillies are wrinkled, they are often sweeter than the smooth hotter ones.

Lemon grass: remember to bash the thin end before using as this helps to release its citrus flavour.

One pot of good quality chunky tomato salsa (uncooked sauce) and one of houmous: you will never be caught short if you have a loaf of part-baked bread in your freezer and a pot of salsa in your fridge.

Stocking the Freezer

I have just got to include a couple of 'must haves' for the freezer:

A bag of frozen berries: whiz in a food processor with crème fraiche or yogurt for an instant ice cream. Crush and mix with a sorbet or serve with a liqueur or champagne drizzled over the top.

A part-baked loaf of bread: whoever pops in unexpectedly will be more than happy when they smell fresh bread baking and they will be even more delighted to taste fresh, squidgy bread drizzled with olive oil and a little garlic.

Sorbets and good quality ice cream: make a homemade sauce (see pages 202-4) and you have a dessert in ten minutes.

A really good chocolate cheesecake: defrost, cut into squares and serve as a chic alternative to chocolate truffles.

Petit pois: if you don't have time to go to the greengrocer on your way home, you will at least have something sweet and green on your plate for supper. If you fancy a treat, add crème fraiche and fresh herbs before serving.

Puff pastry: seriously, who would make it from scratch when this is available. Life is too short.

Nibbles

We all have friends around for drinks and everyone enjoys a nibble to go with their cold G and T or glass of beer. Whatever the tipple, you should find a nibble here to accompany it. You could always serve a few instead of a starter.

Vodka Spiked Tomatoes (V)

This will definitely give your guests something to talk about.

Serves 4
Preparation time: 5 minutes

16 cherry tomatoes
vodka, chilled

Cut a cross in the top of each cherry tomato, pour a little vodka over each, allowing the alcohol to sink in to the middle of the fruit. Serve in a bowl or deep plate. When you bite into the sweet skin and flesh of the tomatoes the cool vodka shoots straight down your throat.

Pernod Spiked Cherries (V)

Why is it that the simplest recipes are always the best?

Serves 4
Preparation time: 10 minutes

16 cherries
Pernod, chilled

Cut a little hole in the top of each cherry and pull the stones out.
Pour the chilled pernod into the fruit and serve in a shallow bowl.

Olives with Orange and Fennel (V)

The combination of orange and fennel is exquisite, the perfect complement to juicy, slightly bitter olives.

Serves 4
Preparation time: 5 minutes
Cooking time: 1 minute

2tsp fennel seeds
340g jar big, juicy, black olives
75ml (3fl oz) extra virgin olive oil
2 garlic cloves, peeled and sliced
3 strips of orange zest

Dry fry the fennel seeds for a minute, then roughly crush. Combine the olives, oil, garlic, orange zest and fennel seeds. Leave to marinate for a couple of days. Serve with cocktail sticks.

Olives with Rosemary, Garlic and Feta (V)

You don't even need to turn the oven on, just mix the ingredients together and leave for at least 3 hours to allow the flavours to develop.

Serves 4
Preparation time: 5 minutes (plus 3 hours resting time)

225g (8oz) olives
75ml (3fl oz) extra virgin olive oil
3 sprigs of fresh rosemary
4 garlic cloves, peeled and sliced
a pack of feta, cubed
salt, freshly ground black pepper

Combine the olives, oil, rosemary, garlic and feta cheese. Leave to marinate for up to a couple of days, the longer the better.

Marjoram Olives (V)

Choose big, black, juicy olives. Put them in a jam jar. Stick a few sprigs of marjoram upright in between the olives and half fill the jar with extra virgin olive oil.

Hot Chilli Olives (V)

Very rarely do we eat olives warm. However, it does make a pleasant change.

Serves 4
Preparation time: 5 minutes
Cooking time: 3 minutes

1 tbsp olive oil
1 red chilli, seeded and chopped
340g jar big, juicy, black olives, stoned

Heat the olive oil in a large wok, add the chilli and sauté for a minute. Add the olives, toss together over the heat for a couple of minutes, serve warm.

Chilli Nuts (V)

This is one of my simplest and trendiest nibbles to serve with drinks. The recipe was inspired by a dish in an American restaurant over which the chef had thrown a similar nutty concoction over a crisp green salad. The quantity is quite large. This is deliberate – keep any leftovers in a screw-top jar (for up to 3 weeks) – perfect for hunger pangs or for pepping up green salads or vegetables. I recommend that you use a mixture of brazil and almonds. If you are not sure how much chilli powder to add, cook the nuts to the recipe. If you find that they are not hot enough, heat a little more oil, add more chilli powder and return the nuts to the pan, cook for a few minutes, tossing the nuts to prevent them from burning.

Serves 6 (as a nibble with some spare for rainy days)
Preparation time: 5 minutes
Cooking time: 5 minutes

1tbsp vegetable oil
1-2tsp Kashmiri chilli powder (Bart Spices)
3 bags nuts (approximately 300g (11oz) in total)
3-4tbsp soy sauce (or to your personal taste)
sea salt flakes

Heat the oil in a wok or large frying pan, add the chilli powder and cook for a minute. Add the nuts and toss to coat with the oil and chilli, sauté for a minute. Add the soy to the pan, it will sizzle as it hits the hot nuts. Sauté over a high heat for 3 minutes or until the pan is dry, stirring frequently so that the nuts do not burn. Sprinkle a few sea salt flakes over and leave to cool on kitchen paper (to drain any excess oil). Serve.

Indian Cashew Nuts (V)

This recipe is based on some of the ingredients used at Christmas time in India. I wrote something similar for *Cosmopolitan* once and, as it proved such a big hit, I decided to include it in this book. However, I have made a couple of alterations. So for those of you who tried the original version, see how this recipe compares and, for everyone else, enjoy a quick hot taste of India. . .

Serves 4
Preparation time: 5 minutes
Cooking time: 15 minutes

2tbsp sunflower oil
1tsp black mustard seeds
1tsp cumin seeds
10 curry leaves
300g (11oz) cashew nuts
½tsp ground turmeric
½tsp cayenne pepper
1tsp ground coriander
sea salt flakes
1tsp lemon juice

Preheat the oven to 180°C/350°F/gas mark 4. Heat the oil in a wok or large saucepan, add the mustard seeds, cumin and curry leaves. When the mustard seeds start to pop, add the cashew nuts and remaining spices. Mix everything together and stir fry for 1 minute. Transfer the nuts to a large ovenproof dish and cook for 10 minutes or until the nuts are golden. Add the salt and leave to cool before serving.

Chinese Pecans (V)

Just like the Chilli Nuts, these are too good to resist munching. However, if you can keep a few, they work really well sprinkled on your supper, especially over stir fries or rice-based dishes.

Serves 6 (as a nibble with drinks)
Preparation time: 5 minutes
Cooking time: 15–20 minutes

275g (10oz) large pecan nuts
2tbsp butter
3tsp five spice powder
a large pinch of sea salt

Preheat the oven to 180°C/350°F/gas mark 4. Spread the pecans in a large, shallow ovenproof dish and dot with butter. Bake until the butter melts, about 5 minutes. Remove from the oven and sprinkle with the five spice and salt. Stir to coat. Bake, stirring frequently, until the pecans are toasted and coated in a buttery spicy mixture, which should take between 10 and 15 minutes. Cool before serving.

Spicy Roasted Seeds (V)

Experiment with the quantity of cayenne pepper until you discover the amount to suit you.

Serves 4
Preparation time: 5 minutes
Cooking time: 15-25 minutes

125g (4oz) sunflower seeds
125g (4oz) pumpkin seeds
sea salt flakes
1tsp cayenne pepper
2tbsp light and fruity olive oil

Preheat the oven to 190°C/375°F/gas mark 5. Put the seeds in a roasting dish, sprinkle them with sea salt flakes and cayenne pepper and toss everything together. Pour over a little olive oil and roast in the preheated oven for 15-25 minutes, turning occasionally to ensure the seeds brown evenly. They are ready when they turn golden. Alternatively, toss the seeds in the sea salt and cayenne pepper and dry fry them in a frying pan over a gentle heat until golden.

Puréed Chickpeas with Fresh Lemon and Mint (V)

Another simple dish that combines a few fresh flavours to make a tasty and light dip without turning the oven on. Often, versions of this recipe use a large amount of oil; to keep ours light and hip friendly I've used a combination of oil, lemon juice and water.

Serves 4-6 (depending on how hungry your guests are)
Preparation time: 10 minutes

2 x 420g cans chickpeas, drained and rinsed
2 garlic cloves, peeled
juice of 1 lemon
75ml (3fl oz) olive oil
3tbsp water
salt, freshly ground black pepper
fresh mint

Put the chickpeas, garlic and lemon juice in a blender and process until smooth. Gradually add the oil in a thin stream, keeping the motor running. Then add the water and purée until the chickpeas are smooth. Season with salt and freshly ground black pepper. Transfer to a serving bowl, scatter the mint over the top and serve with fresh vegetables.

Fresh Herb and Lemon Dip with Vegetable Platter (V)

This makes a refreshing change from creamy dips for vegetables and crisps. In fact, it is also a delicious sauce for hot vegetables, especially mashed potato or steamed asparagus spears.

Serves 4
Preparation time: 5 minutes
Cooking time: 10 minutes

125ml (4fl oz) olive oil
25g (1oz) unsalted butter
2 cloves garlic, peeled and finely chopped
1 small bunch parsley, roughly chopped
1 small bunch of coriander, roughly chopped

Heat the oil and butter over a low heat until the butter melts, add the garlic and cook stirring frequently, until tender, about 10 minutes, without allowing the oil to bubble. Add the herbs and serve immediately with a selection of wonderful vegetables. Beets, radicchio, fennel, carrots, red and yellow peppers are my favourites. However, choose what's in season and have fun playing with the different shapes and colours.

Creamy Blue Cheese Dip
with Walnuts

I am a great believer in using only a few ingredients to make something that is quick and delicious and this recipe is a fine example of just that.

Serves 4-6 (depending on what you are serving it with)
Preparation time: 5 minutes

150ml (5fl oz, ¼pint) plain yogurt
50g (2oz) blue cheese
fresh parsley
a handful of walnuts (optional), lightly toasted

Blend the yogurt and cheese together and chill. Serve with fresh parsley and walnuts (if you fancy) on top.

Pimientos Dip with Spicy Poppadoms

This dip makes a welcome change. You may want to add more balsamic vinegar to give it a slightly sharper taste.

Serves 4
Preparation time: 5 minutes
Cooking time: 10–15 minutes

1 x 290g jar antipasto mixed peppers in a tomato dressing (or something similar)
200g (7oz) half-fat soft cheese with garlic and herbs
splash balsamic vinegar
pack of mini poppadoms (cook as many as you feel you will eat – approx 3 per person)
2tsp paprika pepper

Pour the jar of antipasto peppers into a food processor, add the cheese and purée until smooth. Add a splash of balsamic vinegar, transfer to a bowl and chill until needed. Heat the oil in a large pan or wok. Fry 2 or 3 poppadoms at a time. Drain on kitchen paper. Transfer to the oven to keep warm while you fry the others. Sprinkle the paprika over the poppadoms and serve with the dip.

Chèvre with Herbs

I've discovered that people either love or hate goat's cheese. If you are one of the latter, try this recipe with a good creamy soft cheese instead.

Makes approximately 10 cheese balls
Preparation time: 10-15 minutes

300g (11oz) chèvre du berry
40g (1½oz) mixed fresh herbs (chives, chervil, parsley, basil)
extra virgin olive oil
slices of toasted granary bread, to serve

Roll the cheese into small balls (about the size of cherry tomatoes). Finely chop all of the herbs and scatter on a large plate. Roll the cheese balls in the chopped herbs. Put on a plate, cover and refrigerate. Leave at room temperature for 15 minutes before serving, drizzle with a little extra virgin olive oil and serve with strips of toast.

Mango Chutney and Cheddar Balls

These little balls of tangy mango chutney and Cheddar rolled in freshly chopped herbs are really quite presentable. I just had to include them here, because they are quick, a laugh to make and really quite tasty if you use a good cheese and a tasty chutney, not sandwich leftovers.

Makes approximately 10 balls
Preparation time: 10 minutes

150g (5oz) good strong cheddar, grated
75g (3oz) mango or other flavoured chutney of your choice
fresh parsley, roughly chopped or 50g (2oz) walnuts, finely chopped

Combine the cheese and chutney, then divide the mixture into approximately 10 pieces. Shape into little balls. Roll them in the herbs or nuts, cover and chill for 2 hours before serving.

Garlic and Cheese Strips

I still find it difficult to beat the combination of cheese, garlic and hot toast. I've used pitta bread because it's easy to cut dainty strips for nibbling on. But if you have other bread, it will work just as well. Toasted strips of pitta are also great with tapenade and fresh herbs.

Serves 4
Preparation time: 10 minutes
Cooking time: 20 minutes

3 large pieces of pitta bread
4tbsp extra virgin olive oil
25g (1oz) butter
2 garlic cloves, peeled and finely chopped
50g (2oz) of Mozzarella, grated
25g (1oz) Cheddar or 75g (3oz) of either cheese

Preheat the grill to high, cut the pitta bread in half, then cut each half into strips or triangles. Arrange the pitta triangles in a single layer on two baking trays. Grill the pitta until starting to crisp and turn a pale golden colour. Mix together the oil, butter and garlic and drizzle over the bread. Sprinkle both types of cheese on top. Return to the grill for a few minutes until the cheese has melted and the bread is golden and crispy. Serve hot.

Mediterranean Puff Pastry (V)

Necessity is frequently the mother of invention in my kitchen. I often find myself with leftover pastry and there is only so much space in my freezer. So, one night with a block of pastry, very little time, a jar of olive paste and a hungry boyfriend, these crisp spicy things were born and have been reproduced countless times since.

Serves 4
Preparation time: 10 minutes
Cooking time: 15 minutes

a little olive oil
1 x 375g ready-rolled puff pastry sheet
225g (8oz) tapenade
12 black olives, stoned
sea salt flakes

Preheat the oven to 200°C/400°F/gas mark 6. Lightly brush 2 baking sheets with olive oil. Cut the sheet of pastry in half widthways. Spread the tapenade on to one of the pieces, leaving ½ inch (1cm) border all the way around the edge. Thinly slice the olives, scatter two-thirds of them over the tapenade. Brush the edges of the pastry with olive oil and cover with the other piece of pastry. Roll the sandwich gently to seal the pastry pieces together. Cut the pastry lengthways into 1 inch (2.5cm) strips, then cut each strip diagonally into about 5 diamonds. Arrange on the prepared baking sheets, cut the remaining filled slices into smaller pieces and scatter over the top. Cook in the oven for 10 minutes or until the pastry is golden and puffy. Dust with sea salt flakes and serve immediately.

Tomato and Basil Puffs

This is a variation of the previous recipe, using the classic combination of tomato and basil.

Serves 4
Preparation time: 15 minutes
Cooking time: 10 minutes

a little olive oil
1 x 375g ready-rolled puff pastry sheet
5 fresh tomatoes
3tbsp pesto
fresh basil leaves
sea salt flakes

Preheat the oven to 200°C/400°F/gas mark 6. Lightly brush 2 baking trays with olive oil. Cut the sheet of pastry in half widthways. Spread the pesto on to one of the pieces, leaving a ½ inch (1cm) border all the way around the edge. Deseed and finely chop the tomatoes. Scatter two-thirds of them over the pesto. Sprinkle a few basil leaves over the top and brush the edges of the pastry with olive oil. Cover with the other piece of pastry and roll the sandwich gently to seal the pastry pieces together. Cut the pastry lengthways into 1 inch (2.5cm) strips, then cut each strip diagonally into about 5 diamonds. Arrange on the prepared baking sheets. Cook in the oven for 10 minutes or until the pastry is golden and puffy. Dust with sea salt flakes and serve immediately.

Crispy Potato Slices with Chilli Salsa and Sour Cream

If you are in a hurry, spoon the yogurt and salsa on to thick-cut crisps or tortilla instead of cooking the potato slices. These are great for a drinks party as they are slightly more filling than some of the other ideas and they look as though you have gone to a lot of trouble, even though you haven't!

Serves 4
Preparation time: 10 minutes
Cooking time: 20 minutes

400g (14oz) long thin potatoes
sea salt flakes
1 green chilli, deseeded and finely chopped
150g (5oz) Greek-style yogurt
juice and zest of 1 lime
handful fresh coriander leaves
150g (5oz) pot salsa (uncooked tomato sauce)

Preheat the oven to 200°C/400°F/gas mark 7. Cut the potatoes diagonally widthways about ¼ inch (0.5cm) thick. Arrange the potato slices in a single layer on a baking tray and cook for 20 minutes, turning once. Transfer the tray to a preheated hot grill and continue to cook for 3 minutes on each side until the potatoes are golden and crisp. Put on a warm platter. Mix the chilli into yogurt with the lime juice and zest. Stir the coriander leaves (keep a few for garnish) into the salsa. Top each potato slice with a little yogurt, followed by the salsa. Scatter a few coriander leaves over the top. Serve.

Spicy Crispy Vermicelli (V)

This is a bit of fun and it melts in your mouth as you eat it.

Serves 6
Preparation time: 5 minutes
Cooking time: approx 5-10 minutes

oil
rice vermicelli
sea salt flakes
five spice

Preheat the oven to 110°C/225°F/gas mark ¼. Heat about 1cm of the oil in a large wok or deep pan. Test the oil is hot enough by dropping a small piece of rice vermicelli or bread into the oil; if it crisps immediately, the oil is ready. Cook the vermicelli by dropping small amounts at a time into the oil. As soon as it crisps and puffs, remove, drain on kitchen paper and transfer to the oven. When all of the vermicelli is cooked, sprinkle over the sea salt and five spice, toss together and keep warm in the oven until needed.

Beetroot Chips (V)

A perfect dish for using large beetroot. You can make these chips in advance and keep them warm in a low oven.

Serves 4
Preparation time: 10 minutes
Cooking time: 15 minutes

groundnut oil, for deep frying
5 fresh uncooked beetroot
sea salt flakes
fresh thyme (optional)

Preheat an oven to 110°C/225°F/gas mark ¼. Three-quarters fill a saucepan with groundnut oil and heat, taking care not to overheat. Peel the beetroot and slice finely. Test the oil by dropping in one slice, if it sizzles, the oil is the right temperature. Cook the beetroot in batches, moving around for 2 minutes or until crisp. When the chips are ready, remove from the oil and place in a roasting tin lined with kitchen paper and keep warm. Repeat until all the beetroot is cooked. Toss in sea salt flakes and fresh thyme, if using. Serve.

Sesame Toasts

If you are the sort of person who has occasional cravings for hot buttered toast smothered with Marmite, you will absolutely love this nibble. Just remember that Marmite is quite salty, so have a large drink ready.

Serves 4
Preparation time: 5 minutes
Cooking time: 10 minutes

1 small granary loaf, cut into thick slices
butter
Marmite
sesame seeds

Put the slices of bread under a preheated grill and toast one side until golden. Spread the untoasted sides generously with butter, followed by Marmite (to taste). Scatter the sesame seeds over the top and press down with the back of a knife. Return to the grill for a couple of minutes. Press the seeds into the bread again with the back of a knife and cut the slices into large bite-size pieces.

Parmesan Crisps with Salsa

These little Parmesan crisps are great for canapés or for serving with soups or on top of pasta. They are really simple to make but look incredibly effective.

Serves 6
Preparation time: 10 minutes
Cooking time: 5-10 minutes

125g (4oz) Parmesan
4 ripe tomatoes
juice of ½ a lime
extra virgin olive oil
2 spring onions, finely chopped
freshly ground black pepper
handful of fresh coriander, freshly chopped

Preheat the oven to 180°C/350°F/gas mark 4. Finely grate the Parmesan cheese and sprinkle it to form little circles, about 4 inches in diameter, on to baking sheets. Bake them in the oven until the cheese melts and goes golden brown. Leave them on the baking tray for a minute to cool slightly before lifting them on to a plate with a spatula. Rest them over the back of a spoon to encourage them to curl slightly to make little serving dishes. Deseed and roughly chop the tomatoes, mix with the lime juice, a little olive oil, onion and freshly ground black pepper and coriander. Fill each Parmesan crisp with the tomato mixture and serve.

Starters

In my mind, a meal can be a selection of starters or a main course and a dessert or any other combination of the above. If you are like me and you tend to have more of a savoury tooth than sweet, you should enjoy this chapter. I have developed quite a diverse range of starters including my own version of homemade sushi (made with avocado and other fillings); a creamy noodle dish and a few basic but incredibly tasty vegetable-based dishes (which include one with asparagus and one with mushrooms).

When you are entertaining, starters that have the most visual impact are those that can be served on large plates and passed around to the guests. Walking into the room with a big tray of sushi or mini pizzas, or a big glass dish of fresh melon slices tossed in herbs and chilli with wedges of lime piled high in the centre, will always be a talking point. Think visually whenever you are serving the food – for instance, I always feel plain white plates show the food off better – it is amazing what a difference the presentation makes to the taste and enjoyment of a meal.

Vegetarian Sushi (V)

Traditionally sushi is a combination of sour rice and fish, very often including seaweed. Nowadays, it is often a mixture of sour rice, fruits, vegetables and seaweed. You need half an hour to prepare the Japanese rice, but apart from that this sushi is incredibly quick and, believe it or not, very simple. I love little sushi rolls as starter, they are not too filling if you only eat a few and, more importantly, they impress every time. Also, we are fortunate enough to be able to buy ingredients like konbu and nori seaweed, rice wine vinegar, pickled ginger and wasabi from some major supermarkets and even department stores like Habitat. The easiest way to buy wasabi (Japanese horseradish) is in a tube. Squeeze some into a little dish and use for dipping the sushi into, but go carefully, it is incredibly hot.

Makes 30 pieces: serve about 5 pieces as a starter and 10 for a main course, per person
Preparation time: 20 minutes
Cooking time: 15 minutes (plus 15 minutes standing)

450ml (¾pint) water
1 piece dashi konbu seaweed
225g (8oz) Japanese rice for sushi
2tbsp rice wine vinegar
1tbsp caster sugar
pinch sea salt
flesh of 1 avocado
½ cucumber
6 sheets nori seaweed
dark soy sauce, pickled ginger and wasabi, to serve
(Alternative fillings: mango strips, blanched asparagus, thin strips of omelette, strips of carrot, strips of radish)

Put the water, dashi konbu and rice into a large pan. Bring to the boil, remove dashi konbu, cover rice and simmer for 10 minutes. Leave to stand (still covered) for 15 minutes, then transfer to a bowl. In a small bowl, mix together vinegar, sugar and salt. Stir into the rice and leave to cool

Cut the cucumber in half lengthways, scrape out the seeds with a teaspoon, then cut the cucumber into long thin strips. Cut avocado into slices.

Place a nori sheet on a sushi mat and spoon rice over two-thirds of it. Arrange a few strips of cucumber and avocado (or whichever combination you prefer) in the centre of the rice. Pick up the edge of the mat closest to you and roll the nori and filling away from you. Squash the roll to compress the roll of sushi, i.e., to seal the seaweed wrapped around the rice then unroll the mat. Make up more rolls in the same way. Cut each roll into about 5 or 6 pieces. Serve with little dishes of soy sauce, pickled ginger and wasabi.

Baked Figs with Gorgonzola

Pure indulgence, sticky, gooey and rich.

Serves 4
Preparation time: 5 minutes
Cooking time: 10 minutes

8 fresh figs
150ml (5fl oz) double cream
175g (6oz) Gorgonzola, or Stilton

Preheat a hot grill. Cut the figs in half and arrange in an ovenproof dish. Pour over the cream. Scatter the cheese over the top and grill for 10 minutes until the cheese has melted. Serve with a crisp green salad and fresh bread.

Pear and Camembert Tarts

Cheese and fruit, one of those perfect marriages. Talking of which, I would like to dedicate this recipe to my hubby, who ate pear and Camembert tarts for four consecutive nights until I was content with the end result. You could adapt this recipe at Christmas time, using cranberry sauce and Brie and serve it as a vegetarian alternative to turkey.

Serves 4 (or 6)
Preparation time: 15 minutes
Cooking time: 15-20 minutes

1 x 375g ready rolled puff pastry
3 pears, cored and sliced
125g (4oz) Camembert, sliced
freshly ground black pepper
2tsp soft brown sugar
2tbsp Poire de William or brandy
1tbsp roughly chopped fresh flat leaf parsley
1tbsp roughly chopped thyme
1 egg, beaten

Preheat the oven to 220°C/425°F/gas mark 7. Using a saucer, cut 4 x 5 inch (12.5cm) circles (or use a mug to cut out 6 smaller circles) from the pastry and put on a baking sheet. Use a sharp knife to make an identation about a ½ inch around the edge of each circle. Divide the pear slices between the pastry circles. Scatter the cheese slices over the top. Put the sugar and Poire de William in a saucepan and heat gently to dissolve the sugar. Pour over the cheese and pears. Brush the pastry edges with the beaten egg. Bake for 15-20 minutes until the pastry has risen and is golden and the cheese is bubbling. Scatter the herbs over the tarts and serve.

Melon with Berries, Framboise and Fresh Basil (V)

Fresh fruit is always a refreshing way to begin a meal and it helps you to digest the following courses.

Serves 4
Preparation time: 10 minutes (plus 30 minutes chilling)

225g (8oz) mixed fresh berries (such as raspberries and blueberries)
1tbsp golden caster sugar
juice of 1 lime
1 melon of your choice
basil leaves

Put the berries in a bowl. Mix together the sugar and lime juice and pour over the berries. Peel and deseed the melon, cut the flesh into thick chunks and divide between four serving plates. Spoon the berries on to the melon and chill for 30 minutes before serving. Decorate with a few basil leaves.

Melon with Fresh Mint, Coriander Leaves, Hot Chilli and a Squeeze of Lime (V)

The kick of chilli, fresh juicy melon and herbs is a sensational combination.

Serves 4
Preparation time: 10 minutes

1 melon
½ red chilli, deseeded and finely diced
juice of 1 lime
handful fresh mint leaves
handful fresh coriander leaves

Peel and deseed the melon, cut the flesh into thin strips and divide between four large white plates. Mix the chilli with the lime juice and drizzle over. Roughly tear the mint and coriander leaves and sprinkle over the top.

Mixed Leaves with Toasted Seeds (V)

A lot of people say 'less is more' and this starter is a great example of just that.

Serves 4
Preparation time: 10 minutes
Cooking time: 15-25 minutes

a couple of handfuls of spicy roasted seeds
150g (5oz) fresh mixed salad leaves
large handful fresh basil, and flat leaf parsley and rocket
a few splashes balsamic vinegar
2tbsp fruity olive oil

Prepare the roasted seeds as the recipe in the 'Nibbles' Section (page 25). Mix all the leaves and herbs together and divide between four serving plates. Mix together the vinegar and oil and drizzle over the salad. Scatter the seeds over the salad and serve immediately.

Avocado and Orange Vinaigrette (V)

The younger the watercress the less peppery, so if you are in a position to choose, go for the younger leaves so that they do not overpower the dish. Just for the record, avocado is an excellent source of essential fatty acids and vitamins B and E. This dish also *looks* good.

Serves 4
Preparation time: 15 minutes

juice of ½ blood orange
1tbsp light and fruity olive oil
sea salt, freshly ground black pepper
2 blood oranges
2 handfuls watercress
2 avocados

Mix the orange juice, olive oil and seasoning together. With a sharp knife, cut the top and bottom of the oranges, peel the skin and pith away by working your way around the orange cutting from the top down, trying not to take too much orange flesh with the skin. Cut the flesh into thin circles and place on four serving plates. Scatter the watercress over the top. Cut the avocados in half and take out the stones. Peel each half and slice into thin strips. Scatter the avocado slices over the watercress, drizzle over the orange vinaigrette and serve immediately.

Grilled Courgettes with Cream Cheese Pesto

The creamy pesto cheese is divine with the hot courgettes.

Serves 4
Preparation time: 10 minutes
Cooking time: 10 minutes

3 courgettes
2tbsp olive oil
sea salt and freshly ground black pepper
1 small thin French baguette, thickly sliced
2tbsp fresh basil pesto
125g (4oz) cream cheese
fresh basil leaves

Preheat the oven 220°C/425°F/gas mark 7. Trim the ends of the courgettes and slice thinly diagonally. Arrange on a baking tray and brush with olive oil, season and roast for 10 minutes or until just cooked. Toast the bread, mix the pesto with cream cheese and spread thickly over the hot toast. Cover each with a slice or two of the roasted courgettes and top with another spoon of cream cheese pesto and a fresh basil leaf. Serve immediately.

Blue Cheese with Walnuts and Apricots

Choose walnut bread or the best fresh bread from your favourite bakery or supermarket. If you can get a good nutty one, I advise it.

Serves 4
Preparation time: 5 minutes
Cooking time: 10 minutes

8 ripe apricots, halved and stoned
2tsp soft brown sugar
50g (2oz) walnuts
4 thick slices walnut bread
125g (4oz) Stilton or dolcelatte, crumbled
2tbsp walnut oil
1tbsp red wine vinegar
small bag mixed salad leaves

Preheat the grill to hot. Put the apricots, cut side up, on a baking sheet and sprinkle with the sugar. Grill until the fruit starts to caramelize around the edges, approximately 5 minutes. Transfer the apricots to a plate, then scatter the walnuts over the baking sheet. Grill for a few minutes turning frequently until the nuts are golden and toasted all over. Transfer them to the plate with the fruit. Cut the bread into thick slices, toast on one side, scatter the nuts over the other side, followed by the apricots and blue cheese. Return the toast to the grill and cook for a few minutes until the cheese has melted. Cut the toast into smaller pieces. Mix the oil and vinegar together and drizzle over the salad leaves. Serve the salad with the toasts.

Mini Pizzas with Ratatouille and Mozzarella

I am a great believer in buying a ready-made product, then tweaking it by adding other ingredients and making it homemade. Let's face it, we are all busy and don't want to spend too long in the kitchen.

Makes 12 mini pizzas
Preparation time: 5 minutes
Cooking time: 5 minutes

5 slices of a good Italian olive bread
1 can (approximately 420g) ratatouille
1 pack of Mozzarella, cubed
handful of fresh basil leaves
extra virgin olive oil

Preheat the grill. Cut little rounds (squares or triangles) from the Italian bread, place on a baking sheet and grill until golden. Dollop a small spoonful of ratatouille on top of the toast, followed by a couple of cubes of Mozzarella. Put back under a grill for a minute until the cheese has melted. Scatter the basil over the top, drizzle with a little oil and serve immediately.

Garlic Toast with Herbs and Olive Oil (V)

Everyone loves garlic bread, or at least almost everyone. This is such a simple version that I struggled to decide whether it needs a recipe at all, but I decided it is too scrummy and too popular to ignore. If you keep a part-baked loaf in the freezer, place it in the oven to finish cooking, then cut it into thick slices and continue as the recipe.

Serves 4
Preparation time: 5 minutes
Cooking time: 5 minutes

4 thick slices of granary or white bread, toasted
2 cloves of garlic, peeled
2-3tbsp extra virgin olive oil
handful fresh flat leaf parsley and basil, roughly torn

Toast the bread, rub with the garlic cloves, drizzle with oil and scatter over the freshly torn herbs.

Creamy Lemon and Nutmeg Spinach on Noodles

It is quite a continental idea to have the pasta before the main course, so let's pretend we are in Italy for supper.

Serves 4
Preparation time: 10 minutes
Cooking time: 10 minutes

400g (14oz) tagliatelle or egg noodles
2tbsp olive oil
2 shallots, peeled and finely chopped
2 cloves garlic, peeled and crushed
250g (9oz) baby spinach leaves
fresh nutmeg
2tbsp crème fraiche
handful fresh dill, roughly chopped
juice of ½ lemon
sea salt flakes, freshly ground black pepper

Bring a large pan of water to the boil and cook the pasta according to the packet instructions. Heat the oil in a large frying pan or wok, add the shallot and garlic and sauté for a minute without browning the onion. Roughly tear the spinach into the pan and cook for a couple of minutes until the greens have wilted. Grate fresh nutmeg over the top, stir in the crème fraiche, dill (reserve a little for garnish) and lemon juice. Season, add the pasta to the spinach and mix everything together. Serve in little bowls with the remaining fresh dill on top.

Goat's Cheese with Lemon and Orange

I included this recipe in an al fresco article that I wrote for a summer issue of *Cosmopolitan*. It is so successful for a number of reasons: it is easy to do, looks fabulous and tastes simply scrummy. You may prefer the cheese at the end of the meal, but for some reason which I cannot think of, I feel this recipe idea works well served as little slices of the cheese spread on thin strips of fresh pears for a starter.

Serves 6
Preparation time: 5 minutes

125g (4oz) goat's cheese
50ml (2fl oz) extra virgin olive oil
zest of 1 orange, cut into thin strips
zest of ½ lime, cut into thin strips
3 sprigs rosemary
freshly ground black pepper
3 pears

Put the goat's cheese on a large deep plate and top with the zest and sprigs of rosemary. Drizzle over the olive oil and season with freshly ground black pepper. Leave for at least 1 hour before serving – this gives the flavour from the zest and herbs time to infuse in to the cheese. Core the pears and thinly slice. Spread a little cheese over each piece and drizzle with the zesty oil.

Chargrilled Asparagus with Tomato Vinaigrette (V)

Food writer Lindsey Bareham gave me the idea of making a tomato based vinaigrette dressing. The flavour is fabulously intense if you use really ripe tomatoes and the contrasting colours of rich green asparagus and vivid red sauce look stunning.

Serves: 4
Preparation time: 5 minutes
Cooking time: 6 minutes

700g (1½lb) asparagus
extra virgin olive oil
8 medium-sized ripe tomatoes, skinned and roughly chopped
2tsp balsamic vinegar
sea salt flakes, freshly ground black pepper
1 lemon, cut into chunks

Bring a large pan of water to the boil. Trim the tough bottom ends of the asparagus. Parboil the asparagus for 1 minute, just to soften slightly; drain and leave to cool. Heat a little oil in a griddle pan and cook the asparagus for about 5 minutes in the pan, turning often to char evenly. Meanwhile, whizz the tomatoes in a food processor until smooth, add a little balsamic vinegar and season to taste. Divide the asparagus between warm serving plates and drizzle a little of the tomato vinaigrette over the top and around the plate for effect. Serve with wedges of lemon.

Big Fat Field Mushrooms with Garlic and Herbs

A trendy, fast version of garlic mushrooms with lots of juice for mopping up. Personally, I feel fresh mint works really well. For those of you who are not sure, just add a little more fresh parsley instead.

Serves 4
Preparation time: 5 minutes
Cooking time: 10 minutes

50g (2oz) butter
1tbsp olive oil
2 cloves garlic, peeled and finely chopped
2 shallots, peeled and finely sliced
8 big fat field mushrooms
handful fresh flat leaf parsley
small handful fresh mint

Melt the butter with the oil in a large frying pan or wok. Add the garlic and shallots and sauté for a minute. Cut the mushrooms into thick slices, add to the wok, cover and stew for about 5 minutes. Roughly chop the herbs, add to the mushrooms and toss everything together. Serve immediately.

Oven-roasted Vegetables with a Herb Dressing (V)

Use any vegetables for this dish; choose a selection of those in season that offer different flavours, colours and textures. It may take a while to cook, but leave it in the oven and do something else while it roasts away.

Serves 4
Preparation time: 20 minutes
Cooking time: 50 minutes

2 red onions, peeled
4 baby beetroot, peeled
1 each of red, green and yellow peppers, deseeded
4 courgettes
3 garlic cloves
4 baby turnips, halved
250g (9 oz) baby carrots (keep whole)
a bundle of asparagus

For the dressing:
bunch fresh dill
bunch fresh basil
3tbsp extra virgin olive oil
juice of 1 lemon
1 garlic clove, peeled and crushed
sea salt, freshly ground black pepper

Preheat the oven to 200°C/400°F/gas mark 6. Cut the red onion, beetroot, peppers and courgettes into chunks. Put the red onion, beetroot, peppers, and garlic cloves into a roasting pan and drizzle with the oil. Roast for 30 minutes, add the remaining vegetables and continue to cook for 20-25 minutes. To make the dressing, roughly chop the herbs. Mix together all the dressing ingredients in a bowl and whisk. Add the herbs (reserving a few for garnishing); season with sea salt and freshly ground black pepper. Serve the roasted vegetables on large warm serving plates, drizzle the herb vinaigrette over the top and around the plates. Scatter over the reserved herbs and serve.

Soups

As with all recipes in this book, these soups are fresh, simple and unadulterated. If your cooking does not quite match your own gourmet expectations, homemade soup is an excellent place to begin. One of the most exciting things about soup is that it can be made from almost anything, as long as the incredients you begin with are fresh.

A couple of tips to remember: if you are adding dairy ingredients to the soups (like yogurt or cream), allow the liquid to cool slightly first to prevent curdling. Also, some of the soups in this chapter only require a short cooking time; if you cook for much longer than the specified time you are likely to spoil the flavour and texture of the finished result.

Most of these soups have so much flavour that if you don't have time to make stock, or you find yourself without any Swiss Vegetable Bouillon Powder, use water (anything to avoid the artificial flavours so often associated with stock cubes).

There are a couple of recipes in the book for croûtons (see page 86). It is a good idea to make some up to keep in the freezer for those times when you wish to add a handful to a bowl of steaming hot soup (just remember to thaw them first!).

Spinach and Lentil Soup with Fresh Lemon

Whenever possible, allow others to do some of the work and preparation for you; this includes using cans of lentils or beans that do not require soaking or long cooking times. You do need to eat this quite soon after adding the spinach as the pretty green leaves do not improve with age.

Serves 4
Preparation time: 10 minutes
Cooking time: 35 minutes

3 leeks
2tbsp extra virgin olive oil or a light fruit olive oil (whichever you prefer)
3 garlic cloves, peeled and crushed
700g (1lb 10oz) potatoes, peeled and chopped into small pieces
3 bay leaves
2tbsp roughly chopped flat leaf parsley
1litre (1¾pints) vegetable stock (see page 87 or use
Swiss Vegetable Bouillon Powder)
sea salt flakes, freshly ground black pepper
½ litre (18fl oz) water
420g can green lentils
450g (1lb) young leaf spinach
5tbsp lemon juice (or juice of 1 lemon)
1 lemon, cut into wedges

Cut the leeks in half widthways, then cut each piece in half lengthways and each half into thin strips. Heat the oil in a large saucepan or wok, add the leeks and garlic and cook over a medium heat for 12 minutes or until the leeks have started to caramelize. Add the potatoes, bay leaves, herbs and stock, season well and simmer for

20 minutes. Add the water, lentils, spinach and lemon juice to soup, cook for 1 minute. Serve immediately with a little bowl of lemon wedges.

If you prefer smooth soups, you could remove the bay leaves and purée the soup before adding the water, lentils, spinach and lemon juice.

Watercress and Roquefort Soup

Watercress is a good source of vitamins C and B. It also contains sulphur, potassium, calcium, phosphorous, iodine, beta carotene, folic acid and fibre, so it is a good ingredient to use every now and then.

Serves 4
Preparation time: 10 minutes
Cooking time: 30 minutes

25g (1oz) butter
1tbsp olive oil
3 shallots, peeled and sliced
1 stick celery, trimmed and roughly chopped
15g (1½oz) fresh oregano
900ml (1½pints) vegetable stock (see page 87 or use Swiss Vegetable Bouillon Powder)
2 small potatoes, peeled and diced
2 big bunches watercress, destalked
15g (½oz) fresh marjoram
50g (2oz) Roquefort
125ml (4fl oz) double cream
sea salt, freshly ground black pepper

Melt the butter in a large saucepan, add the oil, and sauté the shallots and celery until soft (approximately 5 minutes). Add the oregano, stock and potato, bring to the boil and simmer for 20 minutes. Add the watercress and marjoram to the saucepan, then purée in batches until smooth. Pour back into the saucepan. Crumble the Roquefort into the cream and mix together. Stir this cream mixture into the soup, warm gently, season and serve immediately.

Pumpkin and Rocket Soup

I made this soup on a really cold night and it was so comforting that I have made it many times since. It will always be a favourite of mine as it is one of those perfect recipes that only need a few ingredients. Rocket has its own peppery flavour so you may not need to add any extra pepper, just season to taste with salt.

Serves 4
Preparation time: 15 minutes
Cooking time: 25 minutes

1tbsp extra virgin olive oil
25g (1oz) butter
1 large onion, peeled and thinly sliced
2 garlic cloves, peeled and finely sliced
900g (2lb) pumpkin or a squash of your choice
75g (3oz) young rocket
1litre (1¾pints) vegetable stock (see page 87 or use Swiss Vegetable Bouillon Powder)
4tbsp Greek yogurt
baby rocket leaves, for garnish

Heat the oil and butter in a large saucepan, add the onion and garlic and fry gently for 5 minutes. Cut the pumpkin in half, scoop out the seeds, peel and cut the flesh into bite-size pieces. Add the pumpkin to the pan and stir well. Cook for 5 minutes. Add half of the rocket and all of the hot stock. Season and simmer for 15 minutes or until the pumpkin is tender. Liquidize until smooth. Return to the pan, add the remaining rocket and heat through for a minute. Spoon into four warm bowls, swirl a little Greek yogurt through each portion and scatter a couple of baby rocket leaves over the top.

Yellow Squash Soup with Garlic and Basil

The beauty of this soup is that it looks pretty and is very light. The garlic and basil work well with the squash.

Serves 4
Preparation time: 15 minutes
Cooking time: 15 minutes

2tbsp olive oil
2 cloves garlic, peeled and finely chopped
6 yellow summer squash
450ml (15fl oz) vegetable stock (see page 87 or use Swiss Vegetable
Bouillon Powder)
450ml (15fl oz) water
6 large ripe tomatoes, diced
Sea salt, freshly ground black pepper
Lots of fresh basil leaves

Heat the oil in a large saucepan, add the garlic and sauté for a minute. Cut the squash into small cubes. Put the squash, stock, water and tomatoes into the saucepan and bring to the boil. Reduce the heat and simmer for 10 minutes. Season with sea salt and freshly ground black pepper. Roughly tear the basil leaves and scatter over the top. Serve.

Gazpacho

I thought it would be nice to include a gazapacho recipe and this one really is a joy to eat. The flavours are so fresh in an uncooked soup and no vitamins and minerals have been lost.

Serves 4
Preparation time: 30 minutes

550g (1¼lb) ripe tomatoes, peeled and finely chopped
200g (7oz) fresh white breadcrumbs
1 medium cucumber, peeled, deseeded and finely chopped
2 cloves garlic, peeled and chopped
1 red pepper, deseeded and chopped
1 orange pepper, deseeded and chopped
4tbsp rice wine vinegar (or white wine vinegar)
5tbsp extra virgin olive oil
1 x 350g jar Cirio's Rustica chopped tomatoes
1tbsp tomato purée
sea salt, freshly ground black pepper
Tabasco sauce

To garnish:
2 hard boiled eggs, peeled and chopped
3 spring onions, finely sliced
6 black olives, stoned and chopped
flat leaf parsley, roughly chopped

In a large bowl, mix together the tomatoes, breadcrumbs, cucumber, garlic, peppers, vinegar, olive oil, Rustica chopped tomatoes and tomato purée. Season and add Tabasco sauce to taste. Pureé in batches with 50ml (2floz) water per batch. Transfer to a clean bowl, chill for at least 3 hours before serving. Stir a little more water into the soup to the desired consistency, add a few ice cubes. To serve, divide between six bowls. Serve with little bowls of the garnishes.

Beetroot Soup with Chive Cream

I hope this recipe demonstrates that it is as easy to make your own beetroot soup as it is to choose one from the shop shelves. Hence I have used cooked beetroot to relieve some of the hassle of peeling and chopping the fresh. By adding half the beetroot at the end of cooking, the soup keeps a brilliant vibrant colour.

Serves 6
Preparation time: 20 minutes (plus 2 hours' chilling time)
Cooking time: 25 minutes

50g (2oz) butter
4 cloves garlic, peeled and chopped
1 carrot, peeled and cubed
1 onion, peeled and chopped
2 plum tomatoes, peeled and roughly chopped
1tbsp white wine vinegar
2tsp mustard powder
1tbsp granulated sugar
2 medium potatoes, peeled and cubed
1.7litres (3pints) vegetable stock (see page 87 or use Swiss Vegetable Bouillon Powder)
450g (1lb) cooked beetroot
sea salt, freshly ground black pepper

For the chive cream:
6tbsp soured cream
handful fresh chives
sea salt, freshly ground black pepper

Heat the butter in a saucepan and fry the garlic, carrot and onion for 5 minutes. Add tomatoes, vinegar, mustard powder and sugar. Cook gently for 5 minutes. Add potatoes, stock and half the beetroot. Season. Bring to the boil and simmer for 15 minutes until the vegetables are soft. Remove from the heat and add remaining beetroot. Liquidize until thick and chunky (not smooth). Chill for 2 hours. Mix the soured cream and half the chives together and season. Serve the soup in big soup bowls or large cups, top with the soured cream mixture and scatter the remaining chives over the top.

Chilled Melon Soup with a Swirl of Raspberry

This makes both an unusual starter and a dessert. I first fell in love with the idea of a fruity soup when I had something similar to this for supper one evening at a friend's restaurant. The rest of the meal was so enjoyable after a light and refreshing soup. It is also really good for the digestion.

Serves 6
Preparation time: 15 minutes
Cooking time: 5 minutes

1 ripe Galia melon, peeled and deseeded
200ml (9fl oz) dry white wine
50g (2oz) granulated sugar
400ml (14fl oz) water
juice and zest of 1 lime
150g (5oz) raspberries (frozen or fresh)

Reserve 75g (3oz) of the melon. Cut the rest into chunks and put in a blender with the wine. Purée until smooth, then pour into a bowl. Dissolve 25g (1oz) of the sugar in the water in a pan over a low heat. Simmer for 5 minutes. Leave to cool. Add sugar syrup and lime juice, a little at a time, to the puréed melon until you are happy with the flavour and texture (this will depend on the sweetness of the melon). Chill for 2 hours before serving into 6 bowls. Purée the raspberries with the remaining sugar and sieve. Swirl the raspberry purée through the soup. Cut the reserved melon into thin strips and pile in the middle of the soup with lime zest on the top.

Cucumber and Walnut Soup

This takes literally about 20 minutes to make with no cooking involved. Just remember to allow 2 hours for chilling. It has got to be the ultimate soup for a cool evening supper al fresco.

Serves 6
Preparation time: 20 minutes

175g (6oz) walnuts
1 large cucumber, deseeded
1tbsp sea salt
450ml pot natural yogurt
2 cloves garlic, peeled and finely chopped
600ml (1pint) vegetable stock (see page 87 or use Swiss Vegetable Bouillon Powder)
50g (2oz) fresh coriander, roughly chopped

Dry fry the walnuts for a couple of minutes until golden, then chop roughly. Reserve ¼ cucumber for garnish, then peel the rest and chop into small pieces. Sprinkle with salt (to draw surplus water from the cucumber) and leave to drain for 30 minutes. Rinse and squeeze out excess moisture on to kitchen paper. Blend the yogurt, garlic, two-thirds of the walnuts and the vegetable stock in a food processor or blender. Add cucumber and blend until smooth. Strain soup through a sieve. Add coriander. Season and chill for at least 2 hours before serving. Thinly slice the reserved cucumber and garnish the soup with cucumber and remaining walnut pieces.

Roasted Sweetcorn Soup with Chilli Oil

Roasting the vegetables brings out their flavour in this soup: the sweetcorn becomes really sweet, the onion takes on a 'meaty onion' flavour and the garlic goes all sweet and sticky. Also, roasting does have the advantage of letting the food cook on its own while you get on with something else.

Serves 4
Preparation time: 20 minutes
Cooking time: 30 minutes

6 ears fresh corn or 500g canned sweetcorn
1 large onion
3 cloves garlic
1 red chilli, halved and deseeded
1 large potato, peeled and cut into small chunks
2tbsp butter
600ml (1pint) vegetable stock (see page 87 or use Swiss Vegetable Bouillon Powder)
125ml (4fl oz) water
2tsp cornmeal
2tbsp olive oil
125ml (4fl oz) Greek yogurt
2 corn tortillas, cut into very thin strips

Preheat oven 220°C/425°F/gas mark 7. Peel the corn husks away from each cob, cut the onion into chunks (keeping the skin on) and put the corn, onion, garlic cloves, chilli and potato on a baking tray. Dot the vegetables with the butter and roast for 30 minutes, then leave to cool. (If using canned sweetcorn, roast all the other vegetables for 20 minutes before adding the corn to the baking tray and continue roasting for 10 minutes). Scrape the kernels away from the cobs. Put the stock and water in a saucepan, squeeze the garlic out of their cases and mix into the saucepan. Add the roasted potato and the onion chunks (peel off the skin first). Add the cornmeal and season the soup to taste. Bring to the boil and simmer for 5 minutes. Add all the corn except a few tablespoons. Purée the soup in batches. Return to the saucepan. Stir in the yogurt (if using) and season to taste. Finely chop the reserved chilli and mix with the reserved corn and oil. Serve the soup in four warm, large white soup bowls. Top with the chilli corn mix and pile a few tortilla strips in the middle. Serve.

Rice Noodle Soup with Lemongrass

Bashing the lemongrass before using helps to release its wonderful citrus flavour.

Serves 4
Preparation time: 10 minutes
Cooking time: 10 minutes

2tbsp olive oil
2 garlic, peeled and sliced
1 inch (2.5cm) piece ginger, peeled and sliced
½ red pepper, deseeded and finely sliced
1 green chilli, deseeded and sliced
2 carrots, thinly sliced
125g (4) oyster mushrooms, roughly torn
250ml (8fl oz) vegetable stock (see page 87 or use Swiss Vegetable Bouillon Powder)
250ml (8fl oz) boiling water
2 stalks lemongrass
sea salt, freshly ground black pepper
200g (7oz) rice noodles
1 lime

Heat the oil in a large pan, add the garlic, ginger, red pepper, chilli, carrots and mushrooms. Soften for a couple of minutes. Add the boiling stock and the water. Bring back to the boil and simmer for 5 minutes. Bash the root end of the lemongrass a couple of times with a rolling pin, add to the soup and season. Add the rice noodles and cook for 5 minutes. Serve with chunks of lime.

Bean Soup with Garlic Oil and Fresh Sage

Serves 6
Preparation time: 10 minutes
Cooking time: 10 minutes

2tbsp olive oil
2 cloves garlic, peeled and finely chopped
handful fresh sage (about 10g), roughly chopped
900ml (1½pints) vegetable stock (see page 87 or use Swiss Vegetable
Bouillon Powder)
2 x 400g cans cannellini beans, drained
sea salt flakes, freshly ground black pepper
50g (2oz) fresh Parmesan
handful fresh flat leaf parsley

Heat the oil in a frying pan, add the garlic and half of the sage and cook very gently without browning the garlic. In a separate saucepan, bring the stock to the boil, add the beans and remaining sage, season and simmer for 5 minutes. Purée the beans in batches until smooth. Return to the saucepan, grate the cheese into large shavings and stir into the soup with the garlic oil. Serve with garlic toasts (see page 63).

Sweet Potato Soup with Lots of Chives and Croûtons

Comfort food in a bowl.

Serves 4
Preparation time: 15 minutes
Cooking time: 30 minutes

1tbsp olive oil
2 shallots, peeled and finely chopped
1 garlic clove, peeled and finely chopped
450g (1lb) sweet potatoes, peeled and roughly chopped
125g (4oz) carrots, peeled and roughly chopped
2tbsp fresh thyme, roughly chopped
sea salt, freshly ground black pepper
568ml (1pint) vegetable stock (see page 87 or use Swiss Vegetable Bouillon Powder)
½ apple, cored and roughly chopped
chopped fresh chives, to garnish
croûtons, to serve

Preheat the oven to 190°C/375°F/gas mark 5. Heat the oil in a frying pan, add the shallots and garlic and fry gently until soft. Stir in the sweet potatoes, carrots, thyme and season. Cover the pan and sweat the vegetables for about 5 minutes. Stir in the stock and apple, bring to the boil and simmer for 20 minutes. Meanwhile, make the croûtons. Chop the bread into cubes and put on a baking tray. Drizzle with olive oil and toss around to coat. Bake for 10 minutes, turning once, until golden brown and crispy. Season. Purée the soup in batches until smooth. Return to the pan and reheat. Serve in warm bowls with fresh chives, and the crunchy croûtons on top.

Vegetable Stock

If you would like to have a go at your own homemade stock, this recipe is simple and well worth making. I have given a recipe for a large quantity as the most sensible thing to do is make up a batch and keep it in the freezer until needed. Just please promise me one thing, you will not use stock cubes instead. The Swiss Vegetable Bouillon Powder is better than a stock cube, but I still feel that homemade is best.

As with all recipes, use good quality ingredients for the quality of the stock will depend on the ingredients you put in it.

Makes 4½ pints (2.6 litres)
Preparation time: 20 minutes
Cooking time: 1 hour 25 minutes

50g (2oz) butter
4 onions, peeled and chopped
5 carrots, chopped
2 leeks, chopped
2 sticks celery, chopped
½ head broccoli, cut into florets
½ head green lettuce
1 bay leaf
handful fresh flat leaf parsley (with stems on)
4 sprigs fresh thyme
sea salt flakes, freshly ground black pepper
6 pints (3.4 litres) water

Put the butter in a large saucepan, heat until melted, add all the vegetables and sweat for 10 minutes over a low heat. Add the rest of the ingredients and bring to the boil. Reduce the heat, partially cover and gently simmer (it is important that the liquid only just bubbles), for 1 hour 25 minutes. Every so often, remove any scum from the top of the liquid. Strain the stock, without pushing any of the vegetables through the sieve. Leave to cool. Refrigerate.

Almost Instant

I feel very strongly that everyone should spend time each day making themselves something to eat. However, I am fully aware that most of us have only a little time available to spend in the kitchen in order to achieve this. With the excellent range of fresh and fast ingredients available nowadays, especially items like couscous, tinned beans, oodles of different noodles, quick polenta and fresh nutty or herb breads, the task has become so much easier. So, whether it is a hot bean spread to go on toast that you fancy or a cinnamon-scented Moroccan couscous dish, there are recipes here that should help you make something tasty to eat in a very short space of time.

Mozzarella and Salsa on Crackers

This salsa, or uncooked, chunky tomato sauce, is seasoned with fennel oil instead of the normal chilli and lime. If you don't have fennel seeds, use crushed chilli flakes or fresh chilli, deseeded and finely chopped.

Serves 4
Preparation time: 10 minutes
Cooking time: 2 minutes

2tbsp olive oil
1tsp fennel seeds, lightly crushed
small handful fresh oregano, roughly chopped
7 vine-ripened plum tomatoes
handful black olives (about 12)
fresh flat leaf parsley
450g (1lb) Mozzarella
½ red onion, peeled and finely sliced
sea salt flakes, freshly ground black pepper

For the salsa, heat the oil in a small pan, add the fennel seeds and heat gently for 1 minute. Remove from the heat and stir in the oregano. Leave to cool. Stir the tomatoes, olives and parsley into the cooled fennel oil. Season. Pop a slice of Mozzarella on the crackers and follow with a spoonful of this salsa and a few onion slices. Serve cold.

Grilled Fig and Gorgonzola Focaccia

Focaccia (Italian bread made with olive oil and available in most supermarkets) has a slightly soft, moist texture and is ideal for using as a base for toppings.

Serves 4
Preparation time: 10 minutes
Cooking time: 10 minutes

1 round focaccia
6 fresh figs
125g (4oz) Gorgonzola, crumbled
fresh rosemary sprigs

Preheat the grill to hot. Cut the focaccia in half horizontally. Slice the figs thinly and arrange on the focaccia. Sprinkle the cheese over the top and scatter a few sprigs of rosemary over the cheese. Put on to baking sheets and toast until the cheese has melted and the figs are slightly browned at the edges. Cut into about 30 squares or slices and serve immediately.

Raw Tomato Sauce with Rocket on Couscous

If you can get hold of fresh, ripe tomatoes, make the most of them by making this quick raw tomato sauce for couscous (or pasta). In my opinion, there is only one other ingredient that has to be included in such a dish and that is fresh rocket. If you want to make this dish even more quickly, use a jar (350g) of Cirio's Rustica crushed tomatoes instead of vine-ripened plum tomatoes.

Serves 4
Preparation time: 10 minutes (plus ten minutes' standing time)

10 vine ripened plum tomatoes
250g (9oz) couscous
sea salt, freshly ground black pepper
50g (2oz) bag fresh rocket
1 clove garlic, peeled and crushed
1tbsp olive oil
50g (2oz) Parmesan shavings (use a vegetable peeler for large shavings)

Cut little crosses in the bottoms of each tomato (this makes it easier to peel them). Boil the kettle, pour boiling water over the tomatoes to cover and leave for 20 seconds (no longer or they will start to cook and go mushy). Drain and plunge straight into cold water for a few seconds, to stop them from cooking, drain. Pour enough boiling water over the couscous to just cover, put cling film over the bowl and leave to stand for 10 minutes. Peel the tomatoes, cut in half and remove the seeds, then roughly chop the flesh into bite-size pieces and put in a bowl. Season with salt and freshly ground black pepper, stir in the rocket (reserving some for a garnish), half of the crushed garlic and olive oil. Fluff the couscous with a fork, add the remaining garlic and Parmesan shavings to the couscous, mix together and season well. Spoon the couscous on to large serving plates, top with the tomato sauce and garnish with fresh rocket.

Avocado with Lime and Coriander on Couscous (V)

It always amazes me just how delightful these little grains of semolina can be with the addition of just a few basic ingredients. Like other carbohydrates the finished flavour is dependent on the other ingredients that you add to them.

Serves 4
Preparation time: 10 minutes

375ml (12fl oz) vegetable stock, boiling (see page 87 or use Swiss Vegetable Bouillon Powder)
250g (9oz) couscous
small handful fresh coriander leaves, chopped
juice of 1 lemon
sea salt flakes, freshly ground black pepper
3 avocados, peeled and sliced
juice of 1 lime
2tbsp extra virgin olive oil
splash Tabasco (to taste)

Pour boiling stock over the couscous to just cover, put a lid or cling film over the top and leave to stand for 5 minutes. Add half the coriander and all the lemon juice to the couscous, season and fluff with a fork to distribute the herbs, leave for another 5 minutes. Cut the avocados in half, remove the stones and slice the flesh. Put the avocado in a large bowl, pour over the lime juice, olive oil and a splash of Tabasco, season well and toss everything together. Spoon the couscous on to four large plates, top with the avocado. Scatter the remaining coriander leaves over the avocados and serve.

Hot Sugared Pears with Roquefort and Rocket

The combination of Roquefort and rocket is excellent.

Serves 4
Preparation time: 5 minutes
Cooking time: 5 minutes

4 pears
25g (1oz) butter
1½tbsp soft brown sugar (unrefined)
fresh coriander leaves
freshly ground black pepper
50g (2oz) bag fresh young rocket leaves
75g (3oz) Roquefort
1tbsp olive oil
½tbsp red wine vinegar

Cut the pears in half, core and slice. Heat the butter in a frying pan, add the brown sugar and coriander and season with freshly ground black pepper. Add the pears and sauté for 2 minutes on each side. Arrange the rocket on four serving plates, crumble the blue cheese over the rocket and top with the hot pear slices. Add the oil and vinegar to the pan, heat through and drizzle the hot juices over the salad, serve.

Poached Egg with Sugar Snap Peas and Fresh Herbs

Imagine the soft gooey egg breaking over crisp, sweet sugar snap peas and creamy mayonnaise melting on top. . .

Serves 4
Preparation time: 10 minutes
Cooking time: 2 minutes (plus standing time)

4 eggs
sea salt flakes, freshly ground black pepper
2tbsp olive oil
2 cloves garlic, peeled and crushed
juice of ½ lemon
75g (3oz) sugar snap peas
100g (4oz) fresh herb salad (available from most supermarkets; alternatively,
mix a selection of herbs such as rocket, watercress, parsley and chives)
handful fresh chives
4dstsp mayonnaise

Poach the eggs: heat a pan of gently simmering water and add a pinch of salt (about ½tsp). Crack the eggs into the water and let them barely simmer for 1 minute. Remove the pan from the heat and leave the eggs in the hot water for 10 minutes. Pour the oil, garlic and lemon juice into a jam jar and shake together. Finely slice the sugar snap peas and mix with the salad. Add the dressing and toss everything together. Arrange on 4 serving plates, placing an egg in the centre of each. Roughly chop the chives, mix into the mayonnaise and spoon on top of each egg. Season with lots of salt and freshly ground black pepper. Serve.

Cannellini Beans with Black Olives (V)

The range of cans of beans available nowadays is just fabulous, but remember to drain and rinse the beans before using as they are often in a salty water solution. This recipe is also delicious with chunks of crumbly feta cheese and a crisp green salad.

Serves 4
Preparation time: 5 minutes

1 clove garlic, peeled
sea salt, freshly ground black pepper
2tbsp extra virgin olive oil
350g jar black olives, stoned and chopped
1tbsp capers, chopped
2 x 400g (14oz) can cannellini beans
juice of ½ lemon

Crush the garlic with a pinch of sea salt flakes in a pestle and mortar and add the olive oil, olives and capers. Crush together to make a slightly lumpy sauce and season. (Alternatively, make this in a food processor by whizzing everything together.) Put the beans, lemon juice and olive sauce in a bowl and mix together well. Season and serve at room temperature.

White Bean Vinaigrette (V)

Drain and rinse a can of cannellini beans, toss in a good vinaigrette and serve on a bed of fresh green salad as an incredibly instant alternative to the previous recipe.

Serves 4
Preparation time: 5 minutes

2 x 400g (14oz) cans cannellini beans
2tbsp red wine vinegar
1tbsp wholegrain mustard
sea salt flakes, freshly ground black pepper
5tbsp extra virgin olive oil
handful fresh mint leaves and flat leaf parsley

Drain and rinse the beans. Shake the vinegar and mustard together in a jar and season. Gradually add the oil and shake again. Pour the vinaigrette over the beans, enough for your taste, and scatter the herbs over the top.

Hot Beans with Tomato (V)

The secret with all of these fast recipes is to use really good quality ingredients and for this one I recommend chopped tomatoes made by Cirio. We are all guilty of sometimes buying the cheaper basic ingredients and then wondering why we are not always happy with the end flavour. If we start to spend a little more on our basics, the finished results are sure to improve.

Serves 4
Preparation time: 5 minutes
Cooking time: 10–15 minutes

1 x 400g (14oz) can of good quality chopped tomatoes or 250g (9oz) fresh
ripe plum tomatoes, deseeded and roughly chopped
sprig fresh rosemary
2tsp tomato purée
1 x 400g (14oz) can cannellini beans, drained
sea salt flakes, freshly ground black pepper
75g (3oz) Parmesan cheese
lots of fresh basil leaves
chunky slices of toast, to serve

Put the tomatoes into a saucepan with the rosemary and tomato purée, simmer for 10 minutes to reduce to a thicker and intense tomato-flavoured sauce. Add the beans, season with salt and freshly ground black pepper and warm through. Grate the Parmesan into large shavings, using a vegetable peeler. Serve the beans in warm bowls, scatter the cheese, with lots of fresh basil leaves over the tops and accompanied by chunky slices of toast.

Indonesian Noodles

Choose a rice or egg noodle for this recipe but, if not, any noodles will work perfectly. Similarly, ring the changes on your choice of vegetables, if you prefer.

Serves 4
Preparation time: 10 minutes
Cooking time: 3 minutes

175g (6oz) egg thread noodles
300g (11oz) carrots
125g (4oz) spring onions

For the dressing:
1tbsp smooth peanut butter
juice of ½ lemon
1tbsp soft brown sugar (unrefined)
1tbsp soy sauce
3tbsp olive oil
1tbsp sesame oil
sea salt, freshly ground black pepper

125g (4oz) beansprouts
200g (7oz) young spinach leaves
2tbsp roughly chopped fresh coriander leaves
2tbsp sesame seeds, toasted (if you fancy)

Bring a large pan of water to the boil, add the noodles, simmer for 3 minutes, drain and rinse. Trim and cut the carrots and spring onions into thin strips. Put all the dressing ingredients in a jar and shake well. Drizzle over the noodles. Add the carrots, spring onions, beansprouts and spinach and toss everything together. Scatter the fresh coriander and sesame seeds, if using, over the noodles and vegetables. Serve.

Linguine with Garlic-infused Oil and Fresh Basil (V)

This is how pasta was served in Italy before tomatoes hit the scene. The recipe gives us an opportunity to appreciate really good extra virgin olive oil (like Carapelli) and fresh garlic (especially new season) and it is perfect for those nights when the cupboard is bare. When cooking the pasta, you need just a large pot, with plenty of water and a little salt. Maintain a rolling boil to allow the pasta to cook freely.

Serves 4
Preparation time: 5 minutes
Cooking time: 10 minutes

400g (14oz) linguine (or pasta of your choice)
200ml (7fl oz) extra virgin olive oil or a fruity olive oil
2 cloves garlic; peeled
handful fresh basil leaves

Bring a large pan of water to the boil and cook the pasta. Drain. Gently warm the oil and garlic in a small pan, without letting the garlic brown, remove from the heat and leave the garlic sitting in the oil for 5 minutes. Remove the garlic and stir the oil into the pasta with the basil. Toss together and serve.

Spaghetti with Chilli, Garlic and Oil

This is a perfect store cupboard supper. You could use chilli powder, or omit it altogether and serve the garlic pasta with cheese and a few fresh herbs.

Serves: 4
Preparation time: 5 minutes
Cooking time: 3 minutes

275g (10oz) spaghetti
2tbsp extra virgin olive oil
3 cloves garlic, peeled and crushed
⅛tsp dried red chilli flakes
50g (2oz) fresh Parmesan shavings

Bring a large pan of water to the boil and cook the pasta according to the packet instructions. Drain. Heat the oil in a frying pan, add the garlic and chilli. Sauté for 3 minutes. Pour over the pasta and mix together. Scatter the cheese over the pasta and serve.

Creamy Parmesan Polenta with Roasted Mushrooms

If you use partly cooked fine cornmeal to make polenta it will take only 10-15 minutes to cook, and the mushrooms and polenta will be ready at the same time. If you prefer pasta to polenta, serve the mushrooms over a pasta of your choice. Alternatively, serve the mushrooms over creamy mashed potato. To be perfectly honest, like a lot of these recipes, they are flexible and really it is up to you to decide how you want to serve them. The only thing I will say is that for vegetarians and meat eaters alike, this dish is filling.

Serves 4
Preparation time: 10 minutes
Cooking time: 15 minutes

375g (13oz) large flat field mushrooms
glug of white wine
75g (3oz) butter
1 clove garlic, peeled and finely chopped
150ml (5fl oz) double cream
fresh nutmeg
sea salt flakes, freshly ground black pepper
175g (6oz) fine cornmeal
750ml (1¼ pint) water
50g (2oz) fresh Parmesan shavings

Preheat the oven to 450°F/230°C/gas mark 8. Put the mushrooms with their caps facing down into a shallow ovenproof dish. Pour a good glug of wine over them, dot half of the butter and all of the garlic on top and season. Cook for 15 minutes so that the mushrooms are cooked and really sizzling, then add the cream and a good grating of nutmeg. Meanwhile, while the mushrooms are in the oven, cook the polenta. This can be done in many ways; check the instructions on the pack as they will vary depending on the fine cornmeal that you are using. The easy-cook polenta can be prepared successfully in this way: put the fine cornmeal in a heavy-based saucepan, gradually add the water, stirring. Bring to the boil, stirring continuously, then simmer, stirring frequently for 5-10 minutes until the mixture is thick and no longer grainy (it should come away from the sides of the pan). Add the remaining butter and most of the Parmesan shavings and season. Divide between four large pasta bowls. Spoon the creamy mushrooms on top and sprinkle with the remaining Parmesan shavings.

Walnut Herb Cream Cheese with Nut Toast

Herbs and nuts mixed into a creamy cheese on crunchy toast is a fabulous combination. If you prefer a less rich mixture, use a little thick natural yogurt with cream cheese instead of mascarpone.

Serves 4
Preparation time: 10 minutes
Cooking time: 5 minutes

75g (3oz) walnuts
2tbsp flat leaf parsley
2tbsp fresh chives
1tbsp tarragon
125g (4oz) mascarpone
250g (9oz) cream cheese
Sea salt, freshly ground black pepper
4 thick slices of fresh hazelnut or walnut bread
2tbsp walnut oil
fresh parsley, chives and tarragon to garnish

Dry fry the walnuts until golden and roughly chop. Beat the herbs into the mascarpone and cream cheese. Stir in the walnuts and season to taste. Toast the slices of bread and drizzle with a little of the walnut oil. Cut the toast into quarters. Arrange on 4 small plates. Spoon dessertspoonfuls of the cheese on to each piece of toast, then pour the remaining walnut oil over the top and garnish with fresh herbs.

Japanese Beetroot Stir Fry
(V)

You may notice that I often use Japanese ingredients in my cooking. They are really wonderful and the great news is they are becoming increasingly easy to find in the shops. The colour from the beetroot in this dish is simply stunning. I could quite happily eat a big bowl of this with a slice of black bread for my lunch, please.

Serves 4
Preparation time: 10 minutes
Cooking time: 10 minutes

1tbsp hazelnut oil
1tbsp groundnut oil
1tbsp pickled ginger
2 leeks, thinly sliced
3 raw beetroot, peeled and grated
1tsp wasabi
3tbsp sake
1tbsp golden granulated sugar

Heat oils in a wok or large frying pan. Add the ginger and leeks and stir fry for 5 minutes. Add beetroot, wasabi, sake and granulated sugar. Stir fry for a few minutes and serve immediately.

Cheshire Cheese with Exotic Fruit

A little taste of the tropics with ripe pawpaw and mango and a good source of both vitamin C and calcium.

Serves 4
Preparation time: 15 minutes

1 small pineapple, peeled
1 avocado, peeled and stoned
1 mango, peeled and stoned
1 pawpaw, peeled and deseeded
125g (4oz) Cheshire cheese
2tbsp olive oil
175ml (7fl oz) orange juice
1tsp coarse grain mustard

Cut all the fruit into bite-size pieces and divide between 4 serving plates. Crumble the cheese over the fruit. In a jam jar, shake together the oil, orange juice and mustard and pour over the salad.

New Zealand Sweet Potato Salad (V)

This recipe was given to me by a friend from New Zealand. She assured me that it is a favourite there, especially in the local delicatessen, and, true enough, it is delicious. The recipe uses the sweet potato found in New Zealand, the kumera, which has the most amazing purple-coloured flesh and skin. The best sweet potato that we can find over here comes from Israel or South Africa. It has an orange flesh and the sugar starts to caramelize as it cooks, creating a delicious vegetable to eat hot, cold or warm.

Serves 4
Preparation time: 10 minutes
Cooking time: 10 minutes

1.1kg (2½lb) sweet potato (kumera), peeled
vegetable oil, for frying
400g (14oz) grapes
150g (5oz) lettuce leaves
150 g (5oz) spinach leaves
4 apples, cored and cut into wedges

For the dressing :
50ml (2fl oz) extra virgin olive oil
juice of 1 lime
sea salt, freshly ground black pepper

Cut the sweet potato into wafer-thin slices. Heat an inch of vegetable oil in a heavy-based pan and fry the sweet potatoes until they are golden brown on each side, about 3-4 minutes. Drain on kitchen paper. In a large salad bowl, toss the sweet potato, grapes, lettuce, spinach and apple wedges together. For the dressing, mix the olive oil and lime juice well and season with sea salt and freshly ground black pepper. Pour over the salad and serve.

Cumin Scented Bean Spread for Hot Toast (V)

Much, much tastier than it sounds. I must admit I do have a passion for cumin; the scent and flavour is simply amazing, especially when you dry fry the seeds and crush them yourself rather than using the powder. This is fab spread thickly over hot toast.

Serves 4
Preparation time: 10 minutes
Cooking time: 2 minutes

2tsp cumin seeds
2 x 400g (14oz) can broad beans and 150ml (¼pint) juice from the cans
1tbsp paprika
½tsp cayenne pepper
5 cloves garlic, peeled
50ml (2fl oz) olive oil
salt and freshly ground black pepper

Dry fry the cumin seeds and crush in a pestle and mortar. Put all the ingredients (except the oil) into a food processor and blend until smooth. Gradually add the oil with the motor running until the mixture is blended. Season with salt and freshly ground black pepper.

Fresh Plum Tomatoes with Feta and Basil

This is a dish that definitely needs to be included in this section. I have eaten it in many guises in a wealth of bistros throughout Europe, which says a lot for its popularity. I always enjoy it, whether as a starter or a main course, but I must stress the importance of choosing fresh, ripe and tasty tomatoes.

Serves 4
Preparation time: 10 minutes

9 vine-ripened plum tomatoes
150g (5oz) feta cheese
2 cloves garlic, peeled and finely chopped
3tbsp extra virgin olive oil
20 big fat and tasty niçoise olives
sea salt flakes
fresh basil leaves

Finely slice the tomatoes or chop into wedges (whichever you prefer) and arrange on four plates. Crumble the milky cheese over the tomatoes and scatter the garlic over the cheese. Pour a little olive oil over each plateful, add the olives and season with little sea salt flakes. Roughly tear the basil leaves and sprinkle them over the top. Serve with chunks of fresh Italian bread.

15 Minutes or Longer

These recipes are all still incredibly quick to prepare, they just take a little longer to cook than those in the previous chapter. The ability to create suppers in a short space of time is all about having clever ideas that turn basic ingredients, like potatoes or lentils, into satisfying suppers. Gorgonzola Mash with a Bowl of Lemon-scented Greens and Lentils with Bananas are both good examples of just that. Also, please don't forget to taste the food as you are cooking. This is especially important when only a few ingredients are being used, as is the case with most of these recipes. If you have added a handful of fresh herbs, taste before adding the second, likewise check the flavour of the dish before adding that third squeeze of lemon juice. Adjust the seasoning to suit you – it's amazing what a difference this can make to the finished dish.

Moroccan Spiced Couscous with Dates, Almonds and Apricots (V)

I have a secret passion for these little grains of semolina, especially prepared with Moroccan flavours. There are many different ways of preparing the precooked couscous: some chefs add hot water or stock, cover and let it stand for 10 minutes. Other chefs believe you end up with a lighter, fluffier couscous if you add cold water or stock, then cover it and leave it to soak in a warm place for about 40 minutes. I would suggest you try both and see which you prefer. More often than not the faster method is more attractive simply because couscous is great to eat as a quick supper dish.

Serves: 4
Preparation time: 5 minutes
Cooking time: 5 minutes

1½tsp cumin seeds
1tsp coriander seeds
2tbsp olive oil
8 spring onions, thinly sliced
1 large clove garlic, peeled and crushed
375ml (12fl oz) vegetable stock (see page 87 or use Swiss Vegetable
Bouillon Powder)
250g (9oz) couscous
1tsp paprika
sea salt flakes
juice and zest of 1 orange
1 red chilli, deseeded and finely chopped
50g (2oz) almonds, roughly chopped
175g (6oz) dried fruits e.g. Medjool dates, apricots and figs, roughly chopped
handful fresh mint and fresh coriander

Preheat the oven to 200°C/400°F/gas mark 6. Dry fry the spices, then crush in a pestle and mortar. Heat half the oil, add half the onion and sauté for 5 minutes until soft. Add the garlic, cook for 1 minute, stir in the ground spices and fry for a minute. Add the stock and bring to the boil and stir in the couscous. Bring to the boil again and stir. Remove from the heat, cover and leave to stand for 10 minutes. Fork the couscous until fluffy, then fork in the rest of the oil. Season to taste with paprika and sea salt flakes. Add the remaining onions and all the other ingredients. Mix together. Cover with foil and bake for 15 minutes. Spoon on to four large serving plates. Scatter the herbs over the top and serve.

Croissants Stuffed with Dolcelatte and Figs

The French croissant dough in a tube is another good product worth keeping in the fridge. Dried figs are an excellent source of fibre – a cupful providing most of the adult daily recommended amount and a quarter of that for vitamin C, riboflavin, vitamn B6, calcium and iron. While this recipe is one idea for using croissant dough to make a tasty supper, you could also try filling the croissants with other ingredients: cream cheese and pesto; Mozzarella and tomatoes; fresh apricot slices or a thick tapenade and chunky olives.

Serves 4
Preparation time: 5 minutes
Cooking time: 20 minutes

1 x 240g pack French croissant dough
5 dried figs
75g (3oz) dolcelatte

Preheat the oven to 200°C/400°F/gas mark 6. Separate the dough triangles along the perforations using a sharp knife. Roughly chop the figs and crumble the cheese. Scatter the figs and cheese over the croissant triangles, loosely roll the croissant dough starting from the broad end of the triangle (making sure that the filling stays inside) to form a croissant shape. Transfer to a baking tray and bake for 20 minutes or until golden and cooked through. Serve immediately.

Spinach and Cream Cheese Sauce for Pasta

Nothing could be simpler, a tasty supper on the table in 15 minutes — or as long as it takes to cook the pasta.

Serves 4
Preparation time: 5 minutes
Cooking time: 15 minutes

400g (14oz) fettuccine or fusilli or pasta of your choice
150g (5oz) cream cheese
50g (2oz) freshly grated Parmesan
150ml (5fl oz) fresh single cream
350g (12oz) baby spinach leaves
freshly ground black pepper and sea salt flakes

Cook the pasta in boiling water according to the pack instructions. Mix the two cheeses together in a saucepan. Add the cream and the spinach leaves and heat through for a few minutes to warm the cream and wilt the spinach. Add the freshly cooked pasta, season well. Serve immediately with fresh herb bread.

Asparagus with a Bright Green Watercress Sauce, with Lightly Boiled Eggs

The yellow in the egg and the vibrant green sauce is a simply stunning colour combination and the contrasting flavours, sublime.

Serves 4
Preparation time: 10 minutes
Cooking time: 10 minutes

4 eggs, at room temperature
900g (2lb) fresh asparagus
40g (1¹/₂oz) fresh watercress
2 spring onions, chopped
3tbsp extra virgin olive oil
juice of 1 lemon
sea salt flakes

Bring a saucepan of water to a gentle simmer. Lower the eggs into the pan and simmer for exactly 1 minute. Remove the saucepan from the heat, put a lid on and leave the eggs for a further 5 minutes. By using this method, you will have a white that is just set with a soft creamy yolk. Then plunge the eggs into cold water to stop them from cooking further. Bring a large pan of water to the boil. Put the asparagus in a wire basket or tie them in a bundle with a piece of string. Immerse the asparagus in the boiling water, cover and cook for 5 minutes. Pierce the thick ends of the stalks with a knife: if they are tender the asparagus is cooked. Put the watercress and onions in a food processor. As the mixture is puréeing, add the oil and lemon juice in a long steady stream and season. Arrange the asparagus on four large warm serving plates. Slice each egg into eight and place over the asparagus with the creamy yolk oozing over the plate. Pour the vibrant green sauce over the egg and asparagus and scatter over a few sea salt flakes. Serve.

Caramelized Leek and Red Onion Frittata

Eaten hot or cold, frittatas are delicious filled with vegetables and cut into wedges, rather like a cake. In this recipe, use milk instead of cream for a lighter frittata, or a combination of both.

Serves 4
Preparation time: 10 minutes
Cooking time: 25 minutes

3 leeks, trimmed
1 red onion, peeled
25g (1oz) butter
1tbsp olive oil
6 eggs
150ml (5fl oz) cream or milk
sea salt flakes, freshly ground black pepper
150g (5oz) soft cream cheese
fresh chives, chopped

Chop the leeks and red onion into thin circles. Heat the butter and oil in a large frying pan and add the leeks and onions. Cook over a medium heat, stirring occasionally, for 10-15 minutes, or until golden brown, soft and caramelized. Put the eggs and cream in a bowl, season well and whisk together. Pour the egg mixture over the onions and cook for about 8 minutes, stirring gently with a spatula – it will still be runny in the centre. Preheat the grill to medium. Dot the cheese over the top and put under the medium grill for 4 minutes, or until golden and firm in the middle. Sprinkle with fresh chives, cut into wedges and serve with a good chutney.

Alternatively, for an Italian version: omit the red onion, use Mozzarella instead of cream cheese and drizzle pesto over the top.

Roasted Tomatoes with a Herb Crust (V)

I do believe that the simple recipes are always the best. There is something really pleasing about this dish – it smells as fabulous as it looks.

Serves 4
Preparation time: 10 minutes
Cooking time: 20 minutes

2 thick slices of white bread
3 garlic cloves, peeled and halved
4tbsp extra virgin olive oil
6 beef tomatoes
225g (8oz) cherry tomatoes
6 plum tomatoes
sea salt, freshly ground black pepper
15g (½oz) fresh oregano
1 small bunch basil leaves
4dstsp mayonnaise

Preheat the oven to 190°C/375°F/gas mark 5. Make the bread into breadcrumbs either by crumbling by hand or whizzing in a food processor. Rub a baking dish with the garlic and reserve the remainder for the crumb topping. Rub the dish with 2tbsp of the oil. Cut a little slit in the top of each tomato. Boil a kettle. Pour boiling water over the tomatoes, leave for 20 seconds before plunging into cold water, drain. Peel the tomatoes (even the cherry tomatoes – it makes such a difference to the finished dish). Cut into thick wedges. Put the tomatoes into the prepared baking dish and season well. Crush the garlic, mix with the breadcrumbs, oregano and remaining oil and sprinkle over the tomatoes. Cook for 20 minutes. Scatter the basil leaves over the cooked dish and serve warm with dollops of mayonnaise.

Noodles with Fresh Ginger and Sesame Oil (V)

Remo Furcas, head chef at Habitat's restaurant in London, gave me this recipe.

Serves 4
Preparation time: 15 minutes
Cooking time: 3 minutes

200g (7oz) egg noodles
4tbsp vegetable oil
4 small aubergines, diced
1 large bunch spring onions
½ inch fresh ginger
3tbsp sesame oil
2 red peppers, deseeded and thinly sliced
2 yellow peppers, deseeded and thinly sliced
1 red chilli, deseeded and thinly sliced
2tbsp rice vinegar
4tbsp soy sauce
bunch fresh coriander leaves, chopped

Bring a large pan of water to the boil, add the noodles and cook for a couple of minutes. Drain. Heat the vegetable oil in a wok and fry the aubergine until golden. Drain on kitchen paper. Trim the spring onions and slice thinly on the diagonal. Peel the ginger and slice thinly. Heat the sesame oil in a wok or large frying pan, add the spring onion, ginger, peppers and chilli. Stir fry for a couple of minutes. Add the vinegar, soy sauce, aubergines and noodles. Toss everything together and serve with the fresh coriander scattered over the top.

Parmesan Courgettes

These are delicious served hot with a crisp green salad. As a starter, just leave out the salad.

Serves 4
Preparation time: 10 minutes
Cooking time: 20 minutes

4 courgettes
6 slices bread
125g (4oz) pine nuts
50 g (2oz) Parmesan cheese
2tbsp roughly chopped parsley
sea salt, freshly ground black pepper
extra virgin olive oil

Preheat the oven to 200°C/400°F/gas mark 6. Cut the courgettes in half lengthways, scoop out the seeds and discard. Whizz the bread into crumbs in a food processor or crumble by hand. Chop the pine nuts and grate the cheese finely. Mix together the crumbs, nuts, cheese, parsley and season. Spoon the breadcrumb mixture into the courgettes, place on a baking tray, drizzle with a little extra virgin olive oil and cook for 20 minutes.

Baby Vegetables in a Coconut Curry Sauce

All this needs is a bowl of steaming fluffy saffron basmati rice to accompany (just add a pinch of saffron to the water when you are cooking basmati).

Serves 4
Preparation time: 10 minutes
Cooking time: 10 minutes

4 shallots, peeled and finely chopped
½tsp turmeric
½ inch fresh root ginger, peeled and chopped
2 stems lemon grass, trimmed
½tbsp red Thai curry paste
1tsp lemon juice
2tbsp groundnut oil
700g (1½lb) fresh vegetables of your choice (I recommend baby corn, sugar snaps, baby carrots)
400ml can coconut milk
200ml (7fl oz) vegetable stock
handful beansprouts
lots of fresh coriander leaves

Put the first 6 ingredients into an electric blender and process to a coarse paste. Heat the oil in a large frying pan or wok. Add the paste and fry until the mixture darkens in colour, adding a drop more oil if required. Add the remaining ingredients, except the beansprouts and coriander, and simmer for 10 minutes, or until the vegetables are tender. Add the beansprouts and cook for another minute. Serve in hot bowls, with lots of fresh coriander leaves scattered over the top.

Bruschetta with Roast Red Peppers (V)

I just had to include a recipe from the wonderful restaurant Terre à Terre' in Brighton, a ground-breaking post-modern vegetarian restaurant with inspirational food. If you find yourselves by the sea in Brighton, it is well worth a visit although, if you are looking to eat there on a Saturday night, you will need to book.

I am often asked the difference between bruschetta and crostini: bruschetta consists of slices of bread, usually sourdough, rubbed with garlic and drizzled with olive oil; crostini is thin slices of bread drizzled with olive oil and baked until crisp and golden.

Serves 4
Preparation time: 10 minutes
Cooking time: 10-15 minutes (grilling peppers)

2 red peppers
50g (2oz) pine nuts
125g (4oz) red onions, peeled
25g (1oz) fine capers
74g (3oz) black olives, stoned
75g (3oz) green olives
225g (8oz) broad beans, cooked and shelled
juice of 1 lemon
2tbsp extra virgin olive oil
1 small bunch basil, roughly torn
4 sprigs fresh thyme
½ small bunch flat leaf parsley, roughly chopped
sea salt and freshly ground black pepper

8 slices of brushetta, or crostini, to serve

Preheat a grill to high, cut the peppers in half and grill until their skins turn black all over. Once charred, if you put the peppers in a sealed plastic bag, the steam helps to loosen the skin. Peel and cut into thin strips. Put the pine nuts on a baking tray and grill for a couple of minutes, turning occasionally, until golden. Dice the red onion and plunge into boiling water for 10 seconds, drain and toss in the lemon juice (watch the red onion turn a beautiful pink colour). Put the pepper strips, onions, capers, olives and beans into a bowl and mix together. Divide between four serving plates. Mix together the lemon juice, oil, herbs and seasoning and pour over the beans and peppers. Scatter the pine nuts over the top. Serve with bruschetta arranged at jaunty angles on each plate. Supply some spoons and forks and away you go!

Gorgonzola Mash with a Bowl of Lemon-scented Greens

The potatoes are unashamedly rich, a perfect complement to the light and lemony greens.

Serves 4
Preparation time: 10 minutes
Cooking time: 20 minutes

For the mash:
900g (2lbs) floury potatoes, peeled and chopped
75g (3oz) butter
75ml (3fl oz) hot milk
175g (6oz) Gorgonzola

For the lemon-scented greens:
1tbsp vegetable oil
4 spring onions, thinly sliced diagonally
450g (1lb) greens like kale, spinach and cabbage, shredded
juice of ½ lemon
sea salt flakes, freshly ground black pepper
1 lemon, cut into wedges

Boil the potatoes until just tender, about 15–20 minutes. Drain and return to the pan, hold them over the heat for a minute to dry. Remove from the heat, add the butter and mash the potato until fluffy. Put the milk in a small saucepan and bring to the boil, then add the cheese and mix well. Stir the cheese mixture into the potato and return to the heat for a minute, still stirring gently. Meanwhile, heat the oil in a wok or large frying pan, add the spring onions and sauté for a couple of minutes. Add the shredded greens and stir fry for a few minutes until they start to wilt. Squeeze the lemon juice over them and season well. Divide the Gorgonzola mash between 4 warm serving bowls, top each with the greens and serve with extra lemon wedges.

Lentils with Fresh Ginger and Madeira with Raita

I have used dried lentils in this recipe rather than tinned because I want the lentils to absorb the flavours from the other ingredients while they cook but, as you can see it is still quick to make. Serve this with raita (see p.126) for a complete meal.

Serves 4
Preparation time: 10 minutes
Cooking time: 25 minutes

1tbsp oil
1 large onion, peeled and thinly sliced
2 carrots, diced
1 bay leaf
2 large garlic cloves, peeled and finely chopped
3-inch piece fresh ginger, peeled and chopped
300g (11oz) green lentils, washed
approximately 600ml (20fl oz) vegetable stock (see page 87 or use Swiss Vegetable Bouillon Powder)
sea salt
2tbsp Madeira wine
juice of ½ lemon
fresh coriander leaves, chopped

For the raita:
200ml (7fl oz) Greek yogurt
¼ cucumber, peeled and coarsely grated
2tbsp fresh mint, chopped
sea salt flakes, freshly ground black pepper

Heat the oil in a large saucepan, add the onion, carrot, bay leaf, garlic and ginger. Cook, stirring occasionally, for 5 minutes. Add the lentils, enough vegetable stock to cover salt and the Madeira. Bring to the boil and simmer for 20 minutes – the lentils should be tender, but not soft. While they are cooking, make the raita: put the yogurt into a bowl, add the cucumber, mint and seasoning. Remove the bay leaf from the lentils, stir in the lemon juice and fresh coriander. Serve in bowls topped with the yogurt raita.

Lentils with Bananas (V)

I could not resist putting this recipe here. It originates from the Canary Islands but I ate something similar in a restaurant in America and I enjoyed it so much, that I created my own version. However, I must say I ate it with grilled fish. If you want to keep it vegetarian serve it with fresh green salad and I am sure you will not be disappointed.

Serves 4
Preparation time: 10 minutes
Cooking time: 7 minutes

25g (1oz) butter
1tbsp olive oil
1 red onion, peeled and cut into wedges
1 clove garlic, peeled and slightly squashed
1 x 400g (14oz) tin puy lentils, drained and rinsed
sea salt flakes, freshly ground black pepper
3tsps balsamic vinegar
3 semi-ripe bananas, peeled and roughly chopped
handful of both fresh coriander leaves and fresh flat leaf parsley

Melt the butter and oil in a large pan, add the red onion and garlic clove. Sauté for about 5 minutes. Add the lentils. Season and pour in the balsamic vinegar. Leave to bubble for a minute then take off the heat. Leave to cool before adding the bananas and herbs. Serve warm or cold.

Angel Hair Pasta in a Lemony Cream Sauce

Capelli d'angelo, or angel's hair pasta, has this name because of its resemblence to long strands of blonde hair. If you can't find it, use the thinnest pasta you can find. Angel hair pasta is also delicious simply tossed in freshly grated Parmesan and melted butter.

Serves 4
Preparation time: 10 minutes (plus standing time)
Cooking time: 10 minutes

250g (9oz) capelli d'angelo pasta
150ml (5fl oz) double cream
zest of 1 large lemon
125g (4oz) French beans
125g (4oz) peas
125g (4oz) asparagus spears, halved
75g (3oz) fresh Parmesan shavings

Heat the cream and lemon zest until it reaches boiling point. Remove from the heat and leave to stand 5-10 minutes (the lemon flavour will infuse the cream). Cook the beans, asparagus and peas 2-3 minutes until tender, then plunge into cold water. Drain and pat dry. Cook the pasta according to the packet instructions and then drain. Mix the lemon cream into the hot pasta with the vegetables. Warm through for a minute, then scatter the Parmesan over the top and serve at once in warm bowls.

30 Minutes or Longer

Instead of spending 30 minutes heating up a supermarket meal, enjoy creating one of these dishes – they are all simple, they do not need huge shopping lists and, more importantly, they are guaranteed to work.

Up in my top ten favourite ingredients of the momennt, along with our friends' couscous and harissa paste, is ready-made fresh or frozen pastry. Who in their right mind is going to spend hours making puff pastry when, in amatter of minutes, they can unroll a sheet, cover it with caramelized onions and mushrooms to make a Mushroom and Caramelized Onion Tart or cut a few circles to make Lime-roasted Tomato Tarts with Rocket Sauce? Also, the availability of fresh vegetables, like sweet potatoes, rocket and many different varieties of tomatoes, make cooking nowadays exciting and easy to do in a short space of time.

Whether it is a puff pastry tart, a slice of a creamy beetroot and tarragon bake or a bowl of steaming chilli and coriander rice that you feel like for supper, I hope you enjoy cooking this really tasty, fresh fast food.

Wild Mushrooms on Creamy Herb Mash

This is very quick as long as you remember to pour boiling water over the dried mushrooms and leave them to soak for 30 minutes before you start to cook. It is also a versatile dish that works just as well with toasted slices of sweet brioche or creamy polenta instead of potato. See page 164 for the creamy herb mash recipe.

Serves 4
Preparation time: 10 minutes (plus 30 minutes' soaking time)
Cooking time: 20 minutes

250ml (8fl oz) boiling water
25g (1oz) dried porcini slices
225g (8oz) flat field mushrooms
225g (8oz) chestnut mushrooms
1tbsp olive oil
25g (1oz) butter
1 clove garlic, peeled and chopped
2 sprigs fresh oregano, chopped
2 drops Tabasco
2 tbsp Madeira
1tsp flour and 1tsp softened butter

Pour the boiling water over the porcini mushrooms and leave to infuse for at least 30 minutes. Meanwhile, boil the potatoes and make the mash according to the recipe on page 164. Lift the slices of porcini out of the bowl and squeeze out the liquor so as not to waste any of the juices. Put the liquor on one side. Roughly chop the porcini into bite-size pieces, chop the flat field mushrooms into long strips and the chestnut mushrooms into chunks. Heat the oil and butter, add the porcini and cook gently for 3 minutes. Add the other mushrooms and cook over a medium heat for 5 minutes. Add the garlic, oregano, Tabasco and the reserved mushroom juice. Cook for another minute before adding the Madeira, then reduce to about half. Mix the softened butter and flour together and stir into the mushroom mixture. Cook for a minute, or until the sauce has thickened slightly. Serve on bowls of creamy herb mash.

Mushroom and Caramelized Onion Tart

Serve this with a fresh green salad for a complete supper.

Serves 4
Preparation time: 10 minutes
Cooking time: 15 minutes

25g (1oz) butter
1tbsp olive oil
2 large onions, peeled and thinly sliced
1 red onion, peeled and thinly sliced
1tbsp freshly chopped thyme
1tbsp freshly chopped parsley
2tbsp balsamic vinegar
250g (9oz) button mushrooms, halved
150g (5oz) baby button mushrooms
150g (5oz) mixed oyster mushrooms, torn into strips
1 x 375g sheet puff pastry, thawed (if frozen)

Melt the butter with the oil in a large frying pan, add the onions and cook stirring occasionally for 10 minutes or until golden and soft. Add the herbs, vinegar and mushrooms and cook for 3 minutes. Place the ready-rolled pastry on a slightly damp baking tray. Top with the onion and mushroom mixture, leaving a 2cm (¾) inch border. Bake in a preheated oven 200°C/400°F/gas mark 6 for 15 minutes or until pastry is golden and puffed.

Lime-Roasted Tomato Tarts with Rocket Sauce

This recipe, which is photographed on the front cover of the book, is definitely one of my favourite vegetarian dishes. It is simple, stylish and easy to make. The combination of crispy pastry, soft and juicy hot tomatoes and a cold, pungent rocket sauce is stunning.

Serves 4
Preparation time: 10 minutes
Cooking time: 25 minutes

225g (8oz) plum tomatoes
2 cloves garlic, peeled
juice of 2 limes
2tbsp extra virgin olive oil
1 x 375g sheet puff pastry, thawed, if frozen

For the rocket sauce:
juice of 1 lime
50g (2oz) fresh rocket
4fl oz (125ml) extra virgin olive oil
50g (2oz) hazelnuts, lightly toasted
fresh rocket, to serve
1 lime, cut into wedges

Preheat the oven to 200°C/400°F/gas mark 6. Pour boiling water over the tomatoes, leave for 20 seconds, drain and peel. Then put them with the garlic into a baking dish, pour over the lime juice and oil, season and cook for 25 minutes. Use a saucer to cut out four 12.5cm (5 inch) circles from the pastry sheet and pierce with a fork. When the tomatoes have only 15 minutes' cooking time left, transfer the pastry to a hot baking tray and bake alongside the tomatoes 10–15 minutes, or until golden and puffy. Whizz all the rocket sauce ingredients together until smooth. Divide the tomatoes between the pastry circles. Pour a little of the rocket sauce over each. Serve immediately with a pile of fresh rocket on top and wedges of limes at the side.

Sweet Potato Chips with Crispy Paprika Onions and Creamy Dressing

Sweet potatoes have a fabulous orange colour and sweet flavour. Oven frying encourages their natural sugars to form a wonderful sticky caramel between the flesh and skin, the result being crisp on the outside and soft in the middle. An alternative way to cook sweet potatoes is to scrub them (do not peel), cover with cold water, bring to the boil and cook for about 20 minutes. Slice thinly, brush with a little olive oil and griddle for a couple of minutes on each side.

Serves 4
Preparation time: 15 minutes
Cooking time: 30 minutes

4-6 sweet potatoes, washed
50g (2oz) butter, melted
75ml (3fl oz) olive oil
sea salt flakes
handful fresh coriander leaves, chopped
4 large Spanish onions, finely sliced
½tsp paprika (and for dusting)
50g (2oz) pistachio nuts
2tbsp Greek yogurt
2tbsp mayonnaise
small handful fresh mint leaves, torn
bag fresh herb salad (available from main supermarkets)

Preheat the oven to 220°C/425°F/gas mark 7. Cut the potatoes in half lengthways, then cut each half into thick slices and put into a bowl. Pour half of the butter and oil over the slices, and toss well to coat. Arrange the slices in a single layer on two baking sheets, season with sea salt and half the coriander leaves over them. Bake 8–10 minutes. Turn the slices over and bake for another 7 minutes or until crisp on the outside and soft in the middle. Meanwhile, heat the remaining oil and butter in a large frying pan and fry the onions with the paprika over a medium heat until crisp, approximately 10 minutes. Dry fry the pistachio nuts for a couple of minutes and roughly chop. Add the remaining coriander and the toasted pistachio nuts to the onion and mix everything together. Mix the yogurt and mayonnaise together. Divide the potato chunks between warm shallow bowls, spoon the crispy onion mixture on top, followed by the mayonnaise mixture. Scatter over some fresh mint leaves, dust with paprika and serve with a herb salad.

Sweet Potatoes with Coriander Salsa and Cream

Marcus and James, my brothers, came over one evening with friends during the testing stage of the recipes in this book. I panicked, thinking that six burly lads would complain if the food was vegetarian. However, I need not have worried. They wolfed this dish down eagerly with not so much as a murmur about the lack of meat. I hasten to add they did still have plenty of room for the Berries with White Chocolate Cream (see page 197) for dessert.

Serves 4
Preparation time: 10 minutes
Cooking time: 30 minutes

4 sweet potatoes
2 red chilli, halved and deseeded
200g (7oz) Greek-style yogurt
juice of 1 lime
15g (½oz) fresh coriander, roughly chopped
sea salt flakes and freshly ground black pepper

Cook the potatoes as described on page 134. Chop the chilli finely and mix into the yogurt with the lime juice. Spoon onto the hot potatoes and scatter over lots of fresh coriander. Season well with sea salt and freshly ground black pepper.

Cream Cheese and Onion Potato Cakes

My grandma was the first person to cook these for me – they are a delight to cook and eat.

Serves 8
Preparation time: 15 minutes
Cooking time: 30 minutes

450g (1lb) potatoes, peeled
2tbsp olive oil
sea salt and freshly ground black pepper
3 spring onions, finely sliced
175g (6oz) fresh chives
60g (2½oz) flour
25g (1oz) butter
125g (4oz) soft cream cheese or Greek yogurt

Roughly chop the potatoes, then bring a large pan of water to the boil. Add the potatoes and simmer for 20 minutes or until tender. Drain thoroughly (they need to be really dry). Return the potatoes to the pan, toss them around over the heat and mash with half the olive oil. Season well, stir in the spring onions, 125g (4oz) of the chives and most of the flour to make a stiff dough. Roll the potato into a large sausage and cut into about 8 thick slices.

Heat the butter and remaining oil in a griddle (or frying pan) and cook the cakes for a couple of minutes on each side. Spoon cream cheese or Greek yogurt on the top of each (it will just begin to melt) and serve after scattering them with the remaining chives.

Spicy Aubergines with Chickpeas

It may take a little longer to leave the aubergines in salt, but it is worth doing as the salt draws the moisture out of the vegetables and stops them from absorbing lots of oil when they are cooked. Cardamom and cinnamon work really well together and especially well with aubergine.

Serves 4
Preparation time: 10 minutes (plus 20 minutes salting the aubergines)
Cooking time: 10 minutes

2 aubergines, roughly chopped
sea salt
4tbsp extra virgin olive oil
3 cloves garlic, sliced
1tsp cardamom seeds, crushed (you will need at least 15 pods to get this many seeds)
1tsp ground cinnamon
1 yellow pepper, halved and deseeded
1 x 400g (14oz) can chickpeas, drained and rinsed
200g (7oz) baby spinach leaves, washed and drained
small handful coriander leaves, chopped

Dressing:
125ml (4fl oz) yogurt
3tbsp fresh mint, roughly chopped
2tsp honey
2tsp cumin seeds, toasted and ground

Put aubergines in a colander, sprinkle with salt and drain for 20 minutes. Make the dressing, mixing together the yogurt, mint, honey and cumin and put to one side. Rinse the aubergines and pat lightly to dry. Heat the oil in a large frying pan, and add the garlic, cardamom and cinnamon. Fry for 1 minute. Thinly slice the yellow pepper, add to the spices with the aubergines. Cook, stirring until golden, for 4 minutes. Add the chickpeas and continue to cook for 2 minutes before adding the spinach and half the coriander leaves. Cook for another 2-3 minutes to wilt the spinach. Divided between 4 warm serving bowls, top with the dressing and scatter the coriander leaves over the top.

Coriander and Chilli Rice with Harissa

Harissa is a paste based on hot red chillies, olive oil and garlic from North Africa – it is now available in good supermarkets.

Serves 4
Preparation time: 15 minutes
Cooking time: approx 30 minutes

1tbsp olive oil
1 onion, peeled and thinly sliced
3 cloves garlic, peeled and roughly chopped
harissa- 1tbsp if you like it hot or 1dstsp
250g (9oz) basmati rice
750ml/1¼pt water
handful fresh coriander (approximately 30g (1¼oz)
1 x 400g (14oz) can sweetcorn
150g (5oz) fresh broccoli, cut into little florets
sea salt, freshly ground black pepper
sour cream
handful fresh coriander leaves, chopped

Heat the oil in a large pan, add the onion and garlic and sauté for 5 minutes. Add the harissa paste and rice. Toss the rice around in the paste to coat. Add the water and coriander. Cover and cook over a low heat for about 10 minutes. Place the sweetcorn and broccoli on top of the rice and continue cooking for another 2 minutes or until the rice is cooked. Leave to sit for a couple of minutes before serving. Season. Garnish with sour cream and coriander.

Saffron Risotto with Butter and Parmesan

Once you know how to cook a risotto properly you will want to cook it again and again. There are so many variations that work well but this is a basic recipe to which you can always add other vegetables and herbs. The dish only takes about 20 minutes to prepare, but you do need to stay with it all the time. The end result should be creamy, shiny and slightly soupy, not mushy.

Serves 4
Preparation time: 10 minutes
Cooking time: 20–25 minutes

large pinch saffron threads
1³/₄ pints (1litre) vegetable stock (see page 87 or use Swiss Vegetable
Bouillon Powder)
50g (2oz) butter
1 small onion, peeled and finely chopped
350g (12oz) arborio rice
75ml (3fl oz) white wine
40g (1¹/₂oz) fresh Parmesan, grated

Dry fry the saffron threads for about 15 seconds. In a pestle and mortar grind the saffron threads to a powder. Put the vegetable stock into a small saucepan and bring to a simmering point (it is important that the stock is kept simmering so that the rice does not stop cooking when the liquid is added to it). Add about 25ml (1fl oz) of the stock to the saffron and leave to infuse. Put half the butter into a heavy-based saucepan (too thin and you may end up with burnt rice) and heat gently. Add the onion and fry until pale golden, not brown. Add the rice and stir for a minute to make sure the rice is really well coated with the butter. Add the wine and let it cook gently until the alcohol has almost evaporated. Begin to add the remaining vegetable stock, a cupful at a time. As the stock is absorbed by the rice, add more. This will take about 20 minutes; you may need to add a little hot water if there is not enough stock. The rice grains should be plump and tender, but still have a little bite. Turn off the heat, add remaining butter and Parmesan cheese, quickly stir everything together, without mashing the rice. Season and serve.

Fajitas

In this dish from Mexico, everyone makes up their own parcels of food, using a warm flour tortilla and lots of other goodies, very often including black beans, chilli and cheese.

Serves 4
Preparation time: 10 minutes
Cooking time: 20 minutes

2 red peppers
1 yellow pepper
8 flour tortillas
1tbsp vegetable oil
1 onion, peeled and finely chopped
2 cloves garlic, peeled and finely sliced
1 red chilli, deseeded and finely sliced
4 plum tomatoes, roughly chopped
2 carrots, grated
1 x 400g (14oz) can sweetcorn
1 x 400g (14oz) can black beans
sea salt, freshly ground black pepper
75g (3oz) Cheddar cheese, grated
baby gem lettuce, finely sliced
150ml (5fl oz) Greek yogurt
fresh coriander leaves, chopped

Preheat a hot grill and an oven to 180°C/350°F/gas mark 4. Put the peppers underneath the grill and cook until the skins are black all over, approximately 10 minutes. Put the peppers into a plastic bag, preferably for 5 minutes (the steam loosens the skin), then peel and cut into strips. Wrap the tortillas in foil and place in the warm oven to heat through for 10 minutes. Meanwhile, heat the oil in a frying pan, and sauté the onion, garlic and chilli for 5 minutes. Add the tomato, carrot, corn, beans and peppers and continue to cook for 10 minutes. Season and stir in the cheese.

To eat, spoon the bean mixture on to each tortilla, scatter a few finely sliced lettuce leaves over the top, followed by a spoon of Greek yogurt and a few coriander leaves. Then fold the sides of the tortilla in to the middle and roll up.

Beetroot, Potato and Tarragon in a Creamy Sauce

This dish looks as scrummy as it tastes. Serve with a fresh green salad for a complete meal.

Serves 4
Preparation time: 15 minutes
Cooking time: 45-50 minutes

1.4kg (3lb) beetroot
450g (1lb) potatoes
2tbsp olive oil
50g (2oz) butter
250g (9oz) Gruyère
sea salt, freshly ground black pepper
handful freshly chopped tarragon (about 3tbsp)
300ml (10fl oz) cream
250ml (9fl oz) milk

Preheat the oven to 180°C/350°F/gas mark 4. Peel the beetroot and potato and chop into chunks. Put the vegetables in an ovenproof dish, drizzle with the oil and roast for 20-30 minutes, until almost tender. Cut the vegetables into smaller, bite-size pieces. Butter another ovenproof dish, place a layer of vegetable pieces along the bottom, sprinkle over a little cheese, season and scatter some of the fresh tarragon over the top. Repeat with another layer of vegetables, cheese and herbs and then continue until all of the vegetables have been used. Mix the cream and milk together, pour over the vegetables and dot with the remaining butter. Bake for 20 minutes, or until the sauce is bubbling and the top is golden.

Koftas in a Spicy Tomato Sauce (V)

These spicy balls are really filling and the sauce quite intense without being overpowering. It is a truly successful little dish.

Serves 4-6
Preparation time: 15 minutes
Cooking time: 25 minutes

For the sauce:
1 large onion, peeled
1tbsp vegetable oil
sea salt, freshly ground black pepper
juice of ½ lemon
1 x 400g (14oz) can chopped tomatoes (a good brand, preferably Cirio)
2tsp tomato purée

For the koftas:
1tbsp cumin seeds
1tbsp vegetable oil, plus enough for shallow frying
200g (7oz) mushrooms, finely chopped
handful fresh coriander
1tsp chilli powder (Bart Spices)
sea salt and freshly ground black pepper
1 x 400g (14oz) can green lentils, drained and rinsed
175g (6oz) breadcrumbs (made from approximately 2 slices of bread)
1tbsp flour and for dusting
handful fresh parsley, chopped

Grate the onion, and heat the oil in a large heavy-based saucepan. Put one tablespoon of the grated onion to one side and sauté the rest until it turns golden brown. Then reduce the heat and season with salt, freshly ground black pepper and the lemon juice. Add the tomatoes and purée to the pan. Simmer for 25 minutes or until the sauce has reduced, making it thick in consistency and intense in flavour.

Meanwhile, make the koftas: heat a frying pan and dry fry the cumin seeds for a minute until they start to go golden in colour. Crush with a pestle and mortar. Heat some of the oil and fry the reserved onion with the mushrooms, crushed cumin seeds and fresh coriander. Add a little chilli, then season with sea salt and freshly ground black pepper. Transfer to a bowl and leave to cool. Add the lentils, breadcrumbs and flour. Mix well. Shape into small balls (makes about 18). Dust well with flour. Heat about 1 inch oil in a large frying pan and shallow fry a few balls at a time for a couple of minutes on each side, until crisp and golden on the outside, they will flatten slightly. Divide the koftas between four warm serving plates. Spoon the sauce over the top. Scatter over the parsley and serve.

Hot Cheese and Tomato Puddings

Everyone loves the classic cheese and tomato combination and this is an alternative way to serve the old favourite. For 6 people, a small pudding each with some fresh vegetables makes a perfectly adequate supper. Alternatively, make 4 slightly larger puddings with a green salad for 4 people.

Serves 4-6
Preparation time: 15 minutes
Cooking time: 25 minutes

25g (1oz) butter (plus extra for greasing ramekins)
2 large onions, peeled and thinly sliced
1 garlic clove, peeled and chopped
1 tbsp roughly chopped chives
175g (6oz) Lancashire cheese, chopped
4 ripe plum tomatoes, skinned and thinly sliced
sea salt, freshly ground black pepper
8 slices bread (focaccia is fabulous)
3 eggs
568ml (1pint milk)

Preheat the oven to 180°C/350°F/gas mark 4. Butter 6 small or 4 large ramekins. Heat the butter in a frying pan, sauté the onion for 10 minutes, until soft. Add the garlic, chives, cheese and tomatoes. Season with salt and freshly ground black pepper. Butter the bread and cut into quarters. Divide half of the bread slices between the ramekins. Cover with half of the cheese and tomato mixture; repeat with the remaining bread and cheese and tomato mixture. Whisk together the egg and milk and pour over the bread and tomato and cheese layers. Put the ramekins on to a baking tray and cook for 25 minutes or until the custard is just set and the tops puffed up and golden. Serve immediately.

Baked Onions with Cream and Fresh Mint

It may seem indulgent to have cream and butter in one dish, but we all need something like this every now and again, and the hot sweet onions with the cream and mint are truly sublime. Don't forget some slices of fresh bread to mop up the juices.

Serves 4
Preparation time: 10 minutes
Cooking time: 30 minutes

450g (1lb) onions
50g (2oz) butter
250ml (9fl oz) vegetable stock (see page 87 or use Swiss
Vegetable Bouillon Powder)
a bay leaf
sea salt and freshly ground black pepper
125ml (4fl oz) double cream
handful fresh mint leaves, chopped
fresh nutmeg
black bread (or any bread of your choice)

Preheat the oven to 200°C/400°F/gas mark 6. Peel the onions and, if they are large, cut into chunks (small ones can be left whole) and put into an ovenproof dish. In a small saucepan, heat the stock until boiling, pour over the onions, add half of the butter and bay leaf and transfer to an ovenproof dish. Cook in the oven 20-25 minutes, until tender. Using a slotted spoon, transfer the onions to another dish. Turn the oven off but put the onions back in to keep warm. Put the pan that the onions cooked in on top of the stove and simmer the onion stock over a medium heat until it is reduced by half (this will take about 4 minutes). Add the remaining butter, season and continue to simmer for about 3 minutes. Add the cream and cook, stirring constantly for another couple of minutes. Add the warm onions and mint, grate a little nutmeg over the top and serve.

Hot Peppers and Tomato with Fresh Lemon (V)

This is inspired by trips to France. It is pretty, fresh and easy to prepare. If you are feeling really hungry, serve with freshly cooked pasta or fresh bread rolls.

Serves 4
Preparation time: 10 minutes
Cooking time: 25 minutes

1 tbsp olive oil
1 large onion, peeled and finely sliced
2 garlic cloves, peeled and roughly chopped
1 aubergine, roughly chopped
1 red pepper, deseeded and cut into pieces
2 yellow peppers, deseeded and cut into pieces
450g (1lb) ripe plum tomatoes, deseeded and roughly chopped
2 courgettes, roughly chopped
handful fresh coriander
handful fresh basil
sea salt and freshly ground black pepper
juice of ½ lemon
1 lemon, cut into wedges

Heat the oil in a large frying pan. Sauté the onion and garlic for 5 minutes. Add the aubergine and peppers and cook for a further 10 minutes. Add the tomatoes, courgettes and half of the herbs and cook for another 10 minutes. Season to taste, squeeze over the lemon juice, stir together, scatter the remaining herbs over the top and serve with lemon wedges.

Warm Olive Oil Scones with Parmesan

This is such an easy supper and it is great fun to make and eat – hot scones straight from the oven, dipped in olive oil and served with a chunk of Parmesan cheese. If you want to make sweet, rather than savoury, scones, omit the herbs, add cinnamon, a pinch of sugar and a few chocolate chunks instead.

Serves 4
Preparation time: 15 minutes
Cooking time: 15 minutes

200g (7oz) self raising flour
½tsp baking powder
½tsp sea salt
small handful fresh parsley and tarragon, chopped
4tbsp extra virgin olive oil
1 medium egg
75ml (3fl oz) milk
40g (1½oz) fresh Parmesan, grated

To serve:
extra virgin olive oil and Parmesan cheese

Preheat the oven to 220°C/425°F/gas mark 7. Sift the flour, baking powder and salt into a bowl. Stir in the herbs and then make a well in the middle. Mix together the oil, egg and milk and pour into the well. Mix everything together, but do not beat. Drop 10 little spoonfuls on to a baking sheet, sprinkle with the grated cheese and bake 10–12 minutes until golden brown and cooked through. Eat warm with a bowl of olive oil for dipping and chunks of Parmesan cheese.

Salads and Vegetable Side Dishes

We need to recognize practical constraints when it comes to cooking fresh vegetable dishes or preparing salads, especially the fact they are impossible to make without access to fresh produce. However, with the major supermarkets stocking so many different fresh fruits and vegetables today, our lives have definitely been made easier. Keep a bag of petit pois or young broad beans in the freezer for those times when you really can't get out to the shops. I must also say that preparing lots of fresh salads has my thumbs up, eat as much raw fruit and vegetables as possible to really benefit from their wonderful nutritive value – any form of cooking will reduce their vitamin and mineral content.

Black Olives with Blood Oranges and Fresh Mint (V)

A little taste of Morocco with lots of vitamin C and iron thrown in for good measure.

Serves 4
Preparation time: 15 minutes

4 blood oranges
250g (9oz) feta
150g (5oz) big juicy black olives, stoned
90ml (3fl oz) extra virgin olive oil
handful fresh mint leaves
sea salt flakes, freshly ground black pepper

Cut off the tops and bottoms of the oranges. Use a sharp knife to remove all the skin and pith, working your way around the fruit from the top to the bottom. Slice the flesh crossways into rounds and arrange on four plates. Crumble the feta over the top. Add the olives and pour over the olive oil. Tear the mint leaves over the top and season. Leave to marinate for at least 1 hour before serving.

Watercress and Tomato

This is a different way of incorporating our peppery friend watercress into our diet. It is also delicious added to stir fries at the end of the cooking time so that the leaves just wilt.

Serves 4
Preparation time: 15 minutes

For the dressing:
3tbsp peanut butter
2 cloves garlic, peeled and roughly chopped
small handful fresh coriander
½ red chilli, deseeded
juice of ½ orange
50ml (2fl oz) vegetable oil

8 ripe plum tomatoes
50g (2oz) fresh watercress
1 red onion, peeled and diced

Put all the dressing ingredients into a blender and blend on high for 2 minutes. Cut the tomatoes into quarters, place in a bowl, roughly tear the watercress over the top and add the red onion. Pour the dressing over the salad.

Watercress and Currant

Adding a little sweetness in the form of currants and honey to the peppery watercress is delicious.

Serves: 4
Preparation time: 10 minutes
Cooking time: 5 minutes

125g (4oz) currants
1tbsp red wine vinegar
1tbsp honey
sprig fresh thyme
2tbsp extra virgin olive oil
50g (2oz) fresh watercress

Heat the currants, red wine vinegar, honey and thyme in a saucepan for a couple of minutes to melt the honey. Transfer to a bowl and leave to cool. Add the extra virgin olive oil, and remove the sprig of thyme. Roughly tear the watercress into another bowl, pour the currant sauce over the top and season with lots of salt and freshly ground black pepper. Toss together and serve.

Thai Cucumber

You need to remove the seeds in the cucumbers to prevent this dish from becoming too wet. Rice wine vinegar is very subtle and carries the flavours from the chilli and coriander really well.

Serves 4
Preparation time: 10 minutes

2 cucumbers
2 fresh red chilli, deseeded and diced
1 red onion, peeled and diced
2tbsp fresh coriander, chopped

For the dressing:
1tbsp rice wine vinegar
1tbsp golden caster sugar
2tbsp olive oil
125g (4oz) roasted peanuts, roughly chopped

Cut the cucumber in half lengthways, scoop out the seeds, use a vegetable peeler to cut long, thin strips. Put the strips of cucumber in a bowl with the chilli, red onion and coriander. Mix all of the dressing ingredients together and drizzle over the salad.

Red Onion and Mango (V)

Prepare the mango just as you would a peach: cut in half widthways, pull apart and remove the stone, then peel and dice the flesh. This is a really refreshing salad and not a drop of oil in sight.

Serves 4
Preparation time: 15 minutes

1 mango
6 tomatoes
1 red onion, peeled and diced
½ green chilli, deseeded and diced
1tbsp roughly chopped fresh coriander
2tbsp white wine vinegar
1 lime, cut into chunks

Slice the mango either side of the stone, peel and dice the flesh. Cut the tomatoes in half, remove the seeds and dice the flesh. Mix the mango and tomatoes with the remaining ingredients and chill until needed. Serve with the chunks of lime.

Rocket with Lots of Herbs and Parmesan Croûtons

It just has to be included, a simple, but important, mixed green salad. If you want to eat this as a main course, add some thick Parmesan croûtons.

Serves 4
Preparation time: 10 minutes

200g (7oz) fresh rocket and spinach
1 small bunch fresh basil
1 small bunch fresh dill
1 cucumber

For the dressing:
2tbsp red wine vinegar
1tsp Dijon mustard
sea salt, freshly ground black pepper
90ml (3fl oz) extra virgin olive oil

For the croûtons:
4 slices white bread
4tbsp olive oil
50g (2oz) fresh Parmesan, grated

Put the prepared leaves in a bowl, add the herbs and toss together. Make the dressing: combine the vinegar and mustard, season and gradually add the oil. Drizzle over the salad.

To make Parmesan croûtons: cut thick slices of white bread. Drizzle olive oil over each slice and cut into cubes. Scatter grated Parmesan over the top of the bread cubes and toss until the cubes are coated with cheese. Bake in a hot oven (200°C/400°F/gas mark 6) for about 10 minutes, turning occasionally, until golden and crispy. Then divide the salad between 4 plates. Scatter the Parmesan croûtons over each salad and serve.

Chillied Sweet Potatoes with Sugar Snaps

Serves 4
Preparation time: 10 minutes
Cooking time: 10 minutes

450g (1lb) sweet potatoes, peeled and chopped into small pieces
1tbsp olive oil
1tsp chilli powder
25g (1oz) butter
150g (5oz) fresh baby spinach leaves
150g (5oz) sugar snap peas

For the dressing:
50ml (2fl oz) white wine
1tbsp olive oil
fresh coriander
sea salt, freshly ground black pepper

Bring a pan of water to the boil, add the sweet potato and cook for 5 minutes, or until just tender and cooked, then drain. Heat the oil in a large frying pan, add the chilli powder and sauté the potato for a couple of minutes, until slightly crisp and golden. Drain on kitchen paper and put into a bowl. Add the butter to the pan. Heat and sauté the sugar snap peas for a minute before adding them to the potato, with the spinach. Mix together. Keeping the pan on the heat, deglaze it with the wine. Add the other dressing ingredients, heat through, then pour over the salad. Season with sea salt flakes and freshly ground black pepper. Serve.

Strawberry with Balsamic Vinegar (V)

A wonderful marriage – syrupy balsamic vinegar with fresh strawberries.

Serves 4
Preparation time: 5 minutes
Cooking time: 2 minutes

50g (2oz) walnuts
½ cucumber
125g (4oz) baby lettuce leaves
175g (6oz) strawberries, hulled and quartered

For the dressing:
1tbsp walnut oil
2tbsp olive oil
2tbsp balsamic vinegar
freshly ground black pepper

Dry fry the walnuts until golden, roughly chop and put into a bowl. Cut the cucumber in half lengthways, scrape out the seeds using a teaspoon, and cut into cubes. Add to the nuts. Roughly tear the lettuce leaves into the bowl, add the strawberries and mix everything together. Put the dressing ingredients into a jar and shake well. Drizzle over the salad. Season with freshly ground black pepper and serve.

Roasted Garlic Mashed Potatoes (V)

Roasting garlic transforms its flavour from being strong and pungent to subtle and sweet. The recipe does really need 2 heads, not 2 cloves, of garlic.

Serves 4
Preparation time: 15 minutes
Cooking time: 30 minutes

2 heads garlic
5tbsp extra virgin olive oil
1 bay leaf
small handful fresh thyme (about 10g (¼oz))
900g (2lbs) potatoes, peeled and roughly chopped
salt and freshly ground black pepper

Preheat the oven to 180°C/350°F/gas mark 4. Cut the heads of garlic in half widthways. Bring a pan of water to the boil, add the garlic and simmer for 7 minutes. Remove with a slotted spoon (keep the water for the potato) and put garlic cut side up on a baking tray. Drizzle with about 3 tbsp of the oil, add the bay leaf and thyme, roast for 30 minutes, or until the garlic is soft. Meanwhile, boil the potatoes in the garlic water, drain and return to the pan over a gentle heat to dry then mash with the remaining extra virgin olive oil. Squeeze the sweet and sticky garlic out of its papery skin and mix into the mash. Season and serve.

Mustard Mash

There are so many ingredients that you can add to mashed potato. Mustard is ideal if you are serving the mash with a mushroom- or tomato-based dish.

Serves 4
Preparation time: 10 minutes
Cooking time: 20 minutes

900g (2lbs) potatoes, peeled and roughly chopped
50g (2oz) butter
50ml (2fl oz) milk
3tbsp crème fraiche
sea salt, freshly ground black pepper
2tbsp Dijon mustard

Boil the potatoes for about 20 minutes (or until tender), drain and return to the pan over a gentle heat for a couple of minutes to dry. Add the butter and mash well. Heat the milk and crème fraiche in a separate saucepan. Add to the mashed potatoes. Season and stir in the mustard.

Lemon and Fresh Mint Mash

This recipe uses a lot of fresh mint to give it a really strong flavour. It's also lovely with fresh parsley instead of fresh mint.

Serves 4
Preparation time: 10 minutes
Cooking time: 20 minutes

900g (2lbs) potatoes
50ml (2fl oz) milk
juice of 1 lemon
75g (3oz) fresh mint, roughly chopped

Boil the potatoes, drain, return to the pan and heat gently to dry. Heat the milk in a separate saucepan, pour over the potatoes and mash. Season well and stir in the lemon juice and fresh mint.

Fresh Asparagus in a Nut Oil Vinaigrette (V)

If you don't have any hazelnut oil, olive oil will do just as well.

Serves 4
Preparation time: 10 minutes
Cooking time: 10 minutes

2tbsp hazelnuts
900g (2lbs) fresh asparagus
4 spring onions, finely sliced
1tbsp white wine or white wine vinegar
1tbsp hazelnut oil
1tbsp olive oil
2tbsp roughly chopped flat leaf parsley

Dry fry the hazelnuts for a couple of minutes until golden. Roughly chop. Cook the asparagus in boiling water for about 4–5 minutes until cooked but still crisp. Drain. Mix together all the remaining ingredients, except for the parsley, and pour over the asparagus. Scatter the hazelnuts and parsley over the top and serve.

Fresh Greens with Soy and Ginger (V)

If you feel like being really healthy, these greens with a few crunchy Parmesan croûtons could be served for a quick lunch.

Serves 4
Preparation time: 5 minutes
Cooking time: 5 minutes

2tbsp vegetable oil
½ inch (1cm) fresh root ginger, peeled and finely chopped
900g (2lb) kale, spinach or cabbage (or a mixture of all three)
about 2tbsp soy sauce (add to your own taste)
freshly ground black pepper

Heat the oil in a wok, add the ginger and stir fry for a minute. Shred the greens and add to the wok. Stir fry for a couple of minutes to wilt the greens before adding the soy sauce. Toss everything together (the greens may spit a little as the soy sauce is added), season with black pepper (you will not need salt as the soy is salty) and serve.

Crispy Seaweed (V)

This is a fun dish that can be served with a main course. I was determined to include it in the book because so many people still think that crispy *seaweed* is just that.

Serves 4
Preparation time: 5 minutes
Cooking time: approx 10 minutes

I small cabbage (e.g. Savoy)
groundnut oil for frying

Shred the cabbage very finely. Heat about 3 inches of groundnut oil in a large deep saucepan and deep fry the cabbage for a few seconds until crisp. Remove with a slotted spoon and drain on kitchen paper. Some people sprinkle sugar over the top which is a nice idea; it works well and brings out the flavour of the vegetable.

Sauteed Sugar Snap Peas

This is definitely one of my favourite ways to cook our sweet friend, sugar snap peas. My mother would cook these as a treat. As she very rarely used butter, they became a memorable dish.

Serves 4
Preparation time: 5 minutes
Cooking time: 5 minutes

3tbsp water
25g (1oz) butter
300g (11oz) sugar snap peas
Sea salt flakes

Heat the water with the butter in a wok or saucepan until the water starts to boil. Add the peas and simmer for a few minutes until the vegetable is cooked. Scatter a few sea salt flakes over to season and serve.

Hot Lettuce with Peas (V)

Serves 4
Preparation time: 5 minutes
Cooking time: 5 minutes

½ iceberg lettuce
175g (6oz) peas
handful fresh mint leaves, roughly chopped
2tbsp olive oil or 25g (1oz) butter
Sea salt flakes, freshly ground black pepper

Shred the lettuce into thin strips. Simmer the peas for a few minutes until cooked. Drain and add the lettuce and fresh mint to the pan with a little olive oil. Heat gently to just wilt the lettuce. Season well and serve.

Sweetcorn and Spinach (V)

Serves 4
Preparation time: 5 minutes
Cooking time: 5 minutes

1tbsp vegetable oil
250g (9oz) baby spinach leaves
200g (7oz) sweetcorn (fresh or frozen (defrosted))
1tsp cayenne pepper
1tsp sea salt flakes
2tbsp lemon juice

Heat the oil in a wok or large frying pan, add the spinach and cook for a couple of minutes, or until it starts to wilt. Add the sweetcorn and cook for another minute. Sprinkle with cayenne pepper, salt and lemon juice over the leaves. Toss everything together and serve.

Pak Choi with Gomasio (V)

My father taught me about this recipe idea after his return from one of his many trips to Japan. It is quite nice for a change to scatter gomasio – a seasoning of crushed toasted sesame seeds with sea salt – over freshly cooked vegetables, I've chosen pak choi but you could try another vegetable of your choice. Use this gomasio or sesame salt instead of sea salt in other vegetable dishes or on hard-boiled eggs. It keeps quite well in a tightly sealed jar in the fridge.

Serves 4
Preparation time: 5 minutes
Cooking time: 5 minutes

5tbsp brown sesame seeds
50-75g (2-3oz) pak choi (allow about ½ per person)
2tsp sea salt flakes

Dry fry the sesame seeds for a couple of minutes until the seeds pop, remove from heat and grind to a powder in a pestle and mortar with the salt. Cut the pak choi into strips lengthways and steam over boiling water for about 5 minutes.

Carrots with Orange and Ginger

Orange and ginger are a wonderful match and what better vegetable to combine these flavours with than carrots?

Serves 4
Preparation time: 5 minutes
Cooking time: 10 minutes

1cm (½ inch) piece fresh root ginger, peeled and grated
25g (1oz) golden caster sugar
175ml (6fl oz) freshly squeezed orange juice
450g (1lb) fresh carrots
25g (1oz) butter
freshly ground black pepper

Put the ginger, sugar and orange juice into a saucepan, heat gently to dissolve the sugar and bring to the boil. Chop the carrots thinly, then add them to the juice and sugar. Simmer for about 5 minutes. Add the butter and continue to cook until the liquid has almost evaporated and the vegetables are left glistening and buttery. Sprinkle with freshly ground black pepper and serve.

Courgettes with Lemon (V)

The flavour of courgettes is definitely better when they have been sautéed rather than boiled.

Serves 4
Preparation time: 10 minutes
Cooking time: 5 minutes

1tbsp oil
1 large onion, peeled and thinly sliced
6 courgettes, coarsely grated (do not peel them)
juice of ½ lemon
handful fresh basil leaves
freshly ground black pepper

Heat the oil in a wok and sauté the onion for 5 minutes. Add the courgettes and stir fry for about 5 minutes. Squeeze over the lemon juice and the basil leaves. Mix together well and season with freshly ground black pepper.

Sautéed Courgettes with Fresh Coriander

If you are looking for a vegetable dish that is even simpler than on p.173 this dish is perfect.

Serves 4
Preparation time: 5 minutes
Cooking time: 2-3 minutes

2tbsp sunflower oil
6 courgettes, coarsely grated (do not peel them)
handful fresh coriander leaves
sea salt flakes, freshly ground black pepper

Heat the oil in a wok, add the courgettes and cook quickly – this should only take about 2-3 minutes. Add the fresh coriander leaves and mix everything together. Season and serve.

Caramelized Leeks with Fresh Herbs

This is so sweet and sticky, it's almost like having a relish. It is simply gorgeous on jacket potatoes as a side dish or stirred into mashed potato. Alternatively, to make it into a main dish, mix through freshly cooked noodles with a little extra olive oil and serve in warm bowls.

Serves 4
Preparation time: 15 minutes
Cooking time: 25 minutes

5 leeks
1tbsp olive oil
25g (1oz) butter
1tbsp soft brown sugar
sea salt flakes, freshly ground black pepper
handful fresh parsley, chopped

Cut the leeks in half lengthways and then widthways. Cut each piece into thin strips. Heat the oil and butter in a large wok, add the leeks and cook for 10 minutes. Sprinkle over the sugar and continue to cook over a medium heat for another 15 minutes. The leeks will be golden and sticky. Season well with sea salt flakes and freshly ground black pepper. Add parsley to the leeks and serve.

Fresh Corn with Chilli Butter

There is something delicious about warm husks of corn with lots of butter and fresh chillies dribbling down your face. Perfect for barbeques.

Serves 4
Preparation time: 10 minutes (plus 15 minutes' soaking time)
Cooking time: 20 minutes

4 husks of corn
75g (3oz) butter, softened
1 small red chilli, deseeded and finely chopped
zest of 1 lime
handful fresh coriander, chopped

Pull back the husks from the corn and remove the threads, then push the husks back on to the corn and tie the ends with string. Soak the corn in water for 15 minutes. Preheat a grill to medium. Grill (or barbeque) for 20 minutes, turning regularly. Mix the butter, chilli, lime zest and coriander together. Pull the husks back from the corn and dollop the chilli butter on to the hot kernels to allow it to melt. Serve.

Puddings

If you are anything like me, you will experience both chocolate cravings as well as healthy and guilt-free mood swings, often in the same evening. There are times when a diet drink or sparkling water justifies that extra helping of chocolate pudding. Also, every now and then you might need a dessert that looks impressive but can be knocked up quickly and simply after work. This section should cover just about every eventuality. If you are in a real hurry, but need that sugar fix, throw together one of the sauces and drizzle it over a cool and creamy ice cream or sorbet.

Mexican Biscuits with Fudge Yogurt and Baked Bananas

An intuitive way to use wheat tortillas (incidentally they must be wheat, not corn) and our great friend, unrefined sugar. Unrefined sugar (Billington's or supermarket's own label) not only has significant amounts of magnesium, calcium, iron and potassium, it also has a rich toffee flavour which, when heated, becomes almost caramel-like. And, when left on top of yogurt, miraculously turns the yogurt into a creamy fudge.

Serves 4
Preparation time: 5 minutes (plus 3 hours' chilling time)
Cooking time: 5 minutes

4 bananas
250g (9oz) thick Greek style yogurt
muscovado sugar (unrefined)
8 small wheat tortillas
golden icing sugar, for dusting
3tbsp dark soft brown sugar (unrefined)

Preheat the oven to 220°C/425°F/gas mark 7. Put the bananas in an ovenproof dish and bake for 15-20 minutes until the skins are black and the fruit is soft when squeezed. Divide the yogurt between four little pots or cups, spoon a thick layer of muscovado sugar over the top of each (about 5mm (¾ inch) thick) and chill for at least 3 hours, the longer the better. For the Mexican biscuits, preheat a grill to high. Cut each tortilla into eight triangles and place on a baking sheet. Dust heavily with icing sugar and sprinkle soft brown sugar over the top. Grill or bake for 3-5 minutes or until golden and crispy. Snip open the bananas lengthways. Spoon a little of the fudgy yogurt along the tops and serve with the crunchy biscuits and the remaining fudgy cream.

Orange and Muscovado Sugar Sticks

These are an alternative to the Mexican biscuits, in the previous recipe, for serving with desserts, especially cream- or yogurt-based ones. Instead of orange zest, try another citrus fruit or a grated spice, like nutmeg or cinnamon.

Serves 4
Preparation time: 15 minutes
Cooking time: 5-6 minutes

3tbsp muscovado sugar
plain flour, to dust
1 x 375g (12oz) thawed, if frozen puff pastry sheet
zest of 1 orange
golden icing sugar, to dust

Preheat the oven to 240°C/475°F/gas mark 9. Dust the work surface with a little of the muscovado sugar and flour, place the pastry on top and scatter over the orange zest. Fold both sides of the pastry into the middle, then fold one half on top of the other. Cut lengthways into 10 thin strips. Turn each strip on to its side, cut side up, and sprinkle over more muscovado sugar. Flatten with your hand, then roll into long thin strips. Cut each strip in half lengthways. Transfer to a baking sheet, dust with a little icing sugar and bake for 5-6 minutes until golden brown. Remove to a wire rack before serving cool.

Chilled Lime Yogurt with Pawpaw

Limes have a wonderful affinity with a number of other fruits, especially pawpaw. This recipe takes squeezing lime juice over the flesh of pawpaw that little bit further and is definitely a dessert for when you are feeling virtuous. You could reduce the sugar slightly and serve at breakfast time, as a serving of fresh fruit is an excellent way to start the day.

Serves 4

Preparation time: 10 minutes (plus 30 minutes' refrigeration time)

juice and zest of 2 limes
500ml (18fl oz) natural Greek yogurt
25g (1oz) golden caster sugar (unrefined)
2 pawpaws

Mix the juice and zest of 2 limes with the yogurt and enough sugar to make it sweet enough for your taste. Divide between four little pots or cups and refrigerate for 30 minutes. Cut the pawpaws in half, scoop out the seeds and cut the flesh into thick slices. Arrange the pawpaw slices on four large plates and squeeze the remaining lime juice over them. Put the little pots of lime yogurt on the plates next to the fruit and serve.

Vanilla and Honey Grilled Figs with Peppered Crème Fraiche

Pepper, an under-rated spice in my opinion, is great with sweet as well as savoury food.

Serves 4
Preparation time: 10 minutes
Cooking time: 2-3 minutes

6 fresh figs
2tbsp honey
50g (2oz) butter
a couple of drops of good vanilla extract (not essence)
approx. 150ml (¼ pint) small pot crème fraiche
1tbsp brandy
black peppercorns, freshly ground

Cut the figs in half widthways and arrange them flesh side up on a baking sheet. Combine the honey, butter and vanilla extract and spread over the cut side of the figs. Pop under a preheated grill and cook for 2-3 minutes until golden. Combine the crème fraiche and brandy. Arrange three fig halves on each plate, dollop the crème fraiche by the side, then freshly grind black peppercorns over the top of the crème fraiche and serve.

Blood Oranges with Cardamom

After a trip on the Spice Trail around Zanzibar I was so inspired that I began to develop a wealth of recipes in which spices play a key part. This was one of the first. This one really needs to be served in plain chunky glass tumblers, or glass bowls, to show off the fabulous blood oranges and the delicate little black cardamom seeds drizzling down over the melting creamy ice cream. If you can get hold of Hill Station's cardamom ice cream I definitely recommend it.

Serves 4
Preparation time: 20 minutes (plus 30 minutes' standing time)
Cooking time: 10 minutes

5 big juicy blood oranges (preferably with orange leaves for garnish)
300ml (10fl oz) Muscat de Rivesaltes (or another similar good dessert wine)
cardamom seeds from 3 green cardamom pods (better than larger brown pods)
75g (3oz) golden caster sugar (unrefined)
1 vanilla bean, split
4 scoops of cardamom or vanilla ice cream (preferably Hill Station's cardamom)

Cut the top and bottom of the oranges and, using a sharp knife, peel the fruit, working your way around from the top to the bottom and making sure you remove the pith as you go. Cut each segment away from the membrane and put the fruit into a bowl. Pour the wine over the top, leave to stand for 30 minutes. Crush the cardamom seeds in a pestle and mortar. Drain the orange-infused wine into a saucepan, add the sugar, cardamom seeds and vanilla bean. Stir over a low heat until the sugar has dissolved. Increase the heat and allow to simmer for 2 minutes. Add the oranges and simmer for a further 3 minutes. Remove the vanilla bean and orange slices.

Spoon the hot orange slices into 4 glass tumblers. Scoop the cardamom or vanilla ice cream on top then drizzle the hot sauce over both. If you are lucky enough to have orange leaves, use one to decorate each dessert.

Berry Soup with Sorbet and Bubbles

This dessert has that rare combination of being superbly healthy (a real injection of vitamin C), as well as providing a dazzling dessert that creates ooohhhss and aaaahhhhs around the dinner table. For the most dramatic visual effect, serve the soup in large white soup/pasta bowls with the sorbet in the middle. Pass the bowls around to the guests before cascading the sparkling wine or champagne over the sorbet so that the guests can take delight in watching the sorbet fizz. For a final flourish, scatter fresh aromatic basil leaves over the soup. This is like being on the stage – you could almost take a bow for this one.

Serves 4
Preparation time: 15 minutes
Cooking time: 15 minutes

200ml (7fl oz) fresh pineapple juice
100ml (3½fl oz) smoothie (buy a good smoothie or make your own using a handful of fresh strawberries, juice of 1 orange and a banana. Whizz in a food processor until smooth)
100ml (3½fl oz) freshly squeezed orange juice
juice of ½ lime
1 star anise pod
2 apples, peeled
350g (12oz) assorted berries (raspberries, blueberries, strawberries)
good sorbet of your choice (lemon/orange/mango all work quite well)
handful fresh basil leaves
150ml (5fl oz) champagne or sparkling wine

Put the pineapple juice, fruit smoothie, orange juice, lime juice and star anise in a saucepan. Core and dice the apples, add to the saucepan. Bring up to the boil and gently simmer for about

15 minutes or until the apple is tender. Transfer to a large bowl to cool. Remove the star anise pod. Divide the soup between four large soup/pasta bowls. Put a couple of scoops of sorbet into the centre of each. Roll the basil leaves into a small cigarette shape and cut into thin strips. Serve the desserts, then take the champagne and pour a few good glugs over each sorbet – the sorbet really fizzes. Scatter the basil over each dish and enjoy with a feeling of triumph.

Hot Brioche and Raspberry Parfait

This is a classic example of an excellent recipe idea that is incredibly quick, but very effective. I call it a parfait because it is not an ice cream, though it behaves like one. It freezes incredibly well and has a very smooth texture. Again, this looks stunning with the soft yellow brioche surrounded by an intensely bright raspberry sauce.

Serves 4
Preparation time: 10 minutes (plus freezing time)
Cooking time: 10 minutes

For the raspberry parfait:
200ml (7fl oz) full fat milk
zest of 2 lemons
175g (6oz) golden caster sugar (unrefined)
225g (8oz) cream cheese
450g (1lb) frozen raspberries, thawed

8 brioche slices or 4 small brioche buns
1tbsp berry liqueur (optional)
fresh raspberries, to decorate (optional)

Put all the parfait ingredients, except the raspberries and 25g (1oz) of the sugar, in a food processor and purée until smooth. Transfer to an ice-cream machine and freeze until smooth. (Alternatively, put the mixture into an airtight container and freeze for 3 hours.) Put the raspberries and remaining sugar into a food processor and whizz until smooth. Drizzle half of the raspberry mixture into the parfait, trying to keep a marble effect, and continue to freeze. (If not using a machine, fold the raspberry mixture into the parfait, cover and return to the freezer until frozen.)

Preheat a grill to medium, arrange the brioche slices, or small buns, on a baking tray and warm gently under the grill for a few minutes, turning once. Sandwich chunks of the parfait between two pieces of warm brioche, or cut a slit inside each small bun and spoon the parfait inside. Stir the liqueur, if using, into the reserved raspberry sauce. Serve on large plates: drizzle the remaining raspberry sauce around the plates and, if you have them, scatter a few fresh raspberries around the buns for a final flourish. Serve.

Banana Tarts with Toffee Cream

The perfect marriage, banana and toffee, in a stylish, quick and simple dessert.

Serves 4
Preparation time: 20 minutes (plus chilling time)
Cooking time: 15 minutes

1 x 375g sheet puff pastry, thawed if frozen
150ml (5fl oz) crème fraiche
150ml (5fl oz) fromage frais
4tbsp soft brown sugar (unrefined)
3 large bananas
melted butter, for brushing
golden icing sugar (Billington's), for dusting

Cut 8 circles out of the pastry using a mug or cup, approximately 10 cm (4 inches) in diameter. Transfer to a baking sheet and prick the surface of each circle. Leave in the refrigerator for 30 minutes. Mix the crème fraiche and fromage frais together and sprinkle the brown sugar over the top. Put in the fridge until needed. Preheat the oven to 220°C/425°F/gas mark 7. Spoon a teaspoon of the crème fraiche mixture on to each pastry circle, keeping the rest to serve with the tarts. Slice the bananas and arrange in circles on top of each tart. Brush each with a little butter and dredge in icing sugar. Bake for 15 minutes or until thoroughly browned. Serve with the remaining crème fraiche mixture which will have become toffee-like.

Filo Tart with Pears and Calvados

Filo pastry, or wafer-thin layers of pastry, is easy to use. The key to success is to keep it covered at all times so that it has no chance of drying out and you need to butter or oil each sheet before baking to make the cooked pastry crisp and light.

Serves 4
Preparation time: 15 minutes
Cooking time: 15–20 minutes

15 filo pastry sheets
125g (4oz) butter, melted
4 pears, cored and finely sliced
2tbsp soft brown sugar (unrefined)
2tbsp Calvados (apple brandy)
200ml (7fl oz) Greek yogurt or crème fraiche
a handful of flaked almonds

Preheat the oven to 190°C/375°F/gas mark 5. Separate the filo sheets, place one of the sheets on a buttered board, and butter. Cover with another sheet; and butter. Continue until all sheets are buttered and sitting in a rectangle stack on a board. Cover with rows of overlapping pear slices, leaving a border of about 1 inch. Brush the fruit with butter and, scatter the sugar over the top. Cut the pear pastry widthways into four thick strips, cut each strip in half diagonally to form two triangles so that you end up with eight triangles in total. Transfer to a baking tray. Pour half of the Calvados over the pastry and bake for 15-20 minutes. Fold the remaining Calvados into the Greek yogurt, or crème fraiche. Dry fry the almonds, if using, scatter over the pear tarts and serve with the Calvados cream.

Caramelized Rum Fruits with Passion Fruit

Just as you need a good chocolate cake recipe in every cookbook, so you also need at least one dessert that can be cooked outside on the barbeque, in a desperate hope that at least a couple of evenings will be suitable for eating al fresco. This is my attempt at a dish that can be prepared in advance, cooked outside and served hot or cold. Whether you end up cooking the fruit, be it on a barbeque or under a grill, I guarantee that you will be transported to the tropics (well, at least in your mind) when you taste the combination of rum, limes and mango, banana, passion fruit etc . . .

Also, I have to say, this does look amazing. Visualize the chunks of colourful fruit with the dark shiny rum sauce around the plate and the seeds and juice from the passion fruit scattered over the top. Need I say more?

Serves 4
Preparation time: 20 minutes (to prepare the fruit)
Cooking time: 5 minutes

125g (4oz) light muscovado sugar
125ml (4fl oz) water
50ml (2fl oz) dark rum
juice of 2 limes
50g (2oz) unsalted butter
fruit of your choice, you will need about 6 in total (a good combination – 1 pink grapefruit, 2 ripe peaches, 1 banana, 1 ripe pawpaw, 1 mango)
2 passion fruit, liquidized
2 limes, quartered

Put the sugar and water in a small saucepan, heat gently until the sugar has dissolved. Add the rum, lime juice and butter. Cook gently to melt. Increase heat and simmer until the liquid has reduced to a syrup. Meanwhile, peel and slice the grapefruit, peaches, banana, pawpaw and mango and thread on to wet skewers. Preheat a grill to high. Brush the fruit with the glaze and grill for a couple of minutes on each side – the rum glaze should start to caramelize and the fruit will be warm without being mushy (or pop them on the barbie if you are outside). Serve the warm fruit sticks on large white plates. Drizzle any remaining rum sauce around the plates. Cut the passion fruit in half and drizzle their juice, with the pips, over the fruit. Serve with lime wedges.

Warm Apple Sauce with Brown Shortcake and Cinnamon-scented Cream

If you like the idea of this recipe but don't want to make the shortbread, just buy a good brand of shortbread or fresh shortcake from a bakery and serve with the apple sauce and cinnamon cream.

Serves 4
Preparation time: 15 minutes
Cooking time: 30 minutes

For the shortbread:
125g (4oz) butter, softened
50g (2oz) soft brown sugar (unrefined)
drop vanilla extract (not essence)
175g (6oz) plain flour

For the apple sauce:
50g (2oz) butter
3 large juicy dessert apples, peeled, cored and grated
fresh nutmeg
2dstsp honey

For the cinnamon cream:
142ml (5fl oz) pot double cream
1 cinnamon stick

fresh mint, to decorate

Make the shortbread: preheat the oven to 180°C/350°F/gas mark 4 and grease a baking tray. Put the butter, sugar and extract into a bowl and beat until creamy. Sift the flour into the butter mixture and mix together. You may need to use your hands to gather the mixture together. Transfer to a lightly floured board and mould into about an 8-inch circle. Put on the greased baking tray, prick all over with a fork and bake for about 30 minutes or until golden. Cool on a wire rack and then break into long jagged pieces.

For the apple sauce: heat the butter in a frying pan, add the apple and cook over a medium heat for 5 minutes. Turn the heat up and cook for a minute to caramelize the apples slightly. Grate fresh nutmeg over the top, drizzle over the honey, stir and warm through.

For the cinnamon cream: put the cream and cinnamon in a saucepan and bring to the boil, remove from the heat, cover and let stand for at least 10 minutes to allow the cinnamon time to infuse.

To serve, put a piece of brown shortbread on to four large plates, spoon apple sauce on top and cover with another piece of shortbread. Spoon the cinnamon cream around the outside and decorate with a mint leaf and a dusting of freshly grated nutmeg.

Pecan Fudgy Bites

Simply scrummy with ice cream or crème fraiche or own their own. These bites are chewy, nutty and fudgy all at the same time. If you have time, toast the pecans first before grinding in a food processor.

Serves 4
Preparation time: 10 minutes
Cooking time: 15 minutes

125g (4 oz) ground pecans
75g (3oz) soft brown sugar (unrefined)
2 large egg whites
½tsp vanilla extract (not essence)

Preheat the oven to 180°C/350°F/gas mark 4. Line 3 baking sheets with baking paper. Mix the ground pecans and sugar thoroughly. Whisk the egg whites until stiff and glossy. Add the nut mixture to the egg whites with the vanilla extract and fold in until evenly blended. Spoon dessertspoons of the mixture on to the prepared sheets, leaving space between them so they can expand slightly. Bake 15-20 minutes until golden and slightly firm. Leave on the baking sheets until cool. Lift off the paper and leave to cool completely.

Cardamom Risotto Pudding with Dates or Chocolate

I have spent a lot of time in Rome and have many fond memories of the city. This particular recipe is an adaptation of one of those memories – I remember being struck by the clever idea of serving a sweet risotto for dessert. As with savoury risotto, always use a proper risotto rice, like arborio, and aim for an end result that is slightly soupy, and creamy, not mushy.

Serves 4
Preparation time: 10 minutes
Cooking time: 20 minutes (approx)

50g (2oz) flaked almonds
5 cardamom pods
750ml (1¼ pints) milk
25g (1oz) soft brown sugar (unrefined)
50g (2oz) butter
125g (4oz) arborio rice
approx 1tbsp orange blossom honey (or enough to taste)
75g (3oz) dates, stoned and roughly chopped or 75g (3oz) a good quality dark chocolate, grated

Dry fry the almonds until golden. Split open the cardamom pods and take out the seeds, throwing away the green pods. Put the milk, sugar and cardamom seeds into a saucepan and heat to simmering point. Melt the butter in a heavy-based saucepan, add the rice and stir to coat the grains. Add a ladleful of the hot milk and stir well. When the rice has absorbed the milk, add another ladleful. Continue until the rice is al dente, that is, cooked but still with a 'bite'. The end result should be creamy, with liquid around the rice. Add enough honey to taste, fold through the chopped dates or chocolate and serve.

Tiny Chocolate Cakes

These little cakes, which are ideal with a cup of espresso coffee, should be puffy and light when they first come out of the oven. As they cool they will sink slightly, but they are still scrummy and incredibly chocolatey when cold. In my opinion, every cookbook should have some sort of chocolate cake and this one just so happens to be light, quick and delicious, with a gooey centre. If you want to be really naughty, serve it in a pool of white chocolate sauce (without the basil) see page 202.

Serves 4-6 (depending on the size of little pot you use)
Preparation time: 15 minutes
Cooking time: 10 minutes

100g (3oz) soft brown sugar (unrefined)
5tbsp butter
160g (5½oz) dark chocolate
pinch salt
5tbsp cocoa
few drops good vanilla extract (not essence)
3 egg whites

Preheat the oven to 200°C/400°F/gas mark 6. Butter 4 little ovenproof pots (you really need stainless steel pots) and sprinkle each with a little of the sugar. Put the butter, chocolate, salt, cocoa and 50g (2oz) of the sugar in a small saucepan. Heat, stirring gently and constantly, until the mixture is smooth and the butter and chocolate have melted. Remove from the heat and stir in the vanilla extract. Leave to cool. In a clean bowl, whisk the egg whites to soft peaks. (I said clean because it is much easier to whisk egg whites if the bowl is completely clean, without any trace of oil or grease. To make sure that it is clean, cut a lemon in half and wipe around the bowl.) Add the remaining sugar and whisk again. Fold 2 tbsp of the egg whites into the cooled chocolate mixture and then fold all of the chocolate mixture into the remaining egg whites. Three-quarters fill each pot and bake in the oven 10-12 minutes, until puffy.

The Ultimate Chocolate Slice

Exceedingly rich – you only need a small piece with a good espresso to get a real kick. It helps to have rice paper underneath simply because you can eat then without having to worry about peeling off the paper. However, if you don't have any rice paper, line the tin with greaseproof paper (but remember to remove it before serving). If there are particular nuts or dried fruits that you like, or sweet biscuits instead of digestive, have a go at substituting them for the recommended ones, keeping the quantities the same.

Serves 4
Preparation time: 15 minutes
Cooking time: 10 minutes (for melting the chocolate and toasting the nuts)

edible rice paper, for lining the tin
50g (2oz) hazelnuts, roughly chopped
50g (2oz) brazil nuts, roughly chopped
225g (8oz) plain chocolate (with high cocoa solids)
125g (4oz) butter
1dstsp golden syrup
225g (8oz) sweet or digestive biscuits, broken
50g (2oz) raisins

Preheat a grill to high. Butter and line the base of a 18cm (7 inch) round cake tin with the rice paper. Put the nuts on a baking tray and put under a preheated grill for a few minutes, tossing around occasionally, or until golden. Break chocolate into a bowl over a pan of gently simmering water. Add the butter and syrup and stir until melted. Stir in the biscuits, nuts and raisins, mix well. Pour into the prepared tin, smooth over the top and refrigerate for at least 4 hours. Break into bite-size chunks and serve with coffee.

Berries and White Chocolate Cream

An amazing combination of flavours that needs to be tasted to be believed.

Serves 4
Preparation time: 10 minutes (plus 30 minutes' refrigeration time)
Cooking time: 5 minutes

450g (1lb) mixed berries, such as raspberries or blueberries)
125g (4oz) white chocolate (good quality eg Lindt Excellence)
250g (9oz) pot mascarpone
250g (9oz) fromage frais
4tsp good quality lemon curd
zest of 1 lemon for the top

Divide half the berries between 4 tumblers. Melt the chocolate with the mascarpone in a saucepan over a gentle heat. Remove from the heat, stir in the fromage frais until smooth and leave to cool slightly. Cover the berries with the chocolate mixture. Dollop a teaspoon of curd into the centre of each dessert, followed by the remaining berries. Refrigerate for 30 minutes before serving. Decorate with lemon zest.

Little Pots of Dark Chocolate with Soft, Sticky Dates

This is all about presentation – the contents speak for themselves and it has got to be my all time favourite simple and stunning dessert. Choose little serving pots to suit your theme, shot glasses work well because they look good and hold just the right amount. Remember to choose a chocolate that has a cocoa butter content of 70% minimum.

Serves 4–8 (depends how you serve them)
Preparation time: 15 minutes
Cooking time: 10 minutes

14 Medjool dates (available from good supermarkets)
25g (1oz) butter
125ml (4fl oz) double cream
125ml (4fl oz) crème fraiche
225g (8oz) dark chocolate
1 egg
pinch salt
2 drops vanilla extract
dark or white chocolate for shavings, to decorate

Stone and roughly chop the dates. Melt the butter in a pan, add the dates and sauté for a few minutes. Transfer to a plate. Put the cream and crème fraiche into the same pan and heat gently. Break the chocolate into small pieces and add to the warm cream. Stir over a gentle heat for a few minutes. Take off the heat and continue to stir until all the chocolate has melted. Lightly beat the egg and add to the chocolate with the salt and vanilla. Return to a gentle heat, stirring until smooth and silky. Divide the sautéed dates between the bottom of the pots and cover with the chocolate mixture. Decorate with chocolate shavings. Serve hot or cold.

Croissants with Chocolate, Cardamom and Crème Fraiche

I had to include a few fun and easy chocolate recipes for those desperate chocolate attacks when all you want is chocolate and you want it . . . now. . .

For this sweet croissant recipe, you could either use bought fresh French croissant dough and bake the croissants from scratch (following the pack instructions) or buy them really fresh from a good bakery.

Serves 4
Preparation time: 10 minutes
Cooking time: 10 minutes

4 green cardamom pods
4 large or 8 small fresh crumbly, flaky croissants
100g (3½oz) bar plain chocolate
4tbsp crème fraiche or thick double cream

Preheat the oven to 180°C/350°F/gas mark 4. Open the cardamom pods, remove the little black seeds and crush the seeds in a pestle and mortar (throw away the green pods). Split open the croissants without breaking them all the way through. Break the chocolate into chunks and put inside the croissants. Add the cardamom seeds and a spoonful of crème fraiche or double cream. Wrap the croissants in foil and bake for 10 minutes. Serve hot.

Cheats' Chocolate Truffles

I do like ideas like this one but would anyone actually do this or would they just grab the cheesecake, cut it into slices and eat. I suppose it all depends on how hungry or desperate for chocolate you are.

a good quality chocolate cheesecake
dark chocolate
good quality cocoa powder

Cut the chocolate cheesecake into bite-size squares. Melt the chocolate in a bowl over a pan of simmering water. Drizzle the chocolate over half the squares in little stripes. Dust the other squares heavily with cocoa powder. Refrigerate and serve on a glass platter with coffee.

Plump Dried Fruits and Nuts in Silky, Dark Chocolate

Choose a selection of your favourite dried fruits – big, juicy apricots and Medjool dates work well. Put these with a few big, fresh brazil nuts and all you need is a little chocolate. You really have a few options here for a sophisticated alternative to dessert, or an after-dessert alternative to truffles!

You could make a dark chocolate sauce (see page 202) and pass a little dish of this around with the fruit and nuts for the guests to dip their fruit and nuts into. Or, on the other hand, you could take a bar of good quality chocolate and melt it in a bowl over a pan of simmering water, stir in 1tbsp rum and half dip the fruit and nuts, leave to set and pass around with a cup of espresso.

Sauces

Milk or Dark Chocolate

125g (4fl oz) milk chocolate or dark chocolate
125ml (4fl oz) double cream

Put the chocolate and cream in a saucepan and heat gently, stirring until the chocolate has melted and you have a smooth sauce.

White Chocolate and Basil

250g (9oz) white chocolate
250ml (9fl oz) double cream

Put the chocolate and cream into a saucepan and heat gently, stirring until the chocolate has melted and you have a smooth sauce. Roll the basil leaves into a cigar shape and thinly slice into strips. Add half to the chocolate sauce. Serve the sauce and scatter the remaining basil leaves over the top.

Toffee

175g (6oz) soft dark brown sugar (unrefined)
225ml (8fl oz) double cream

Put the ingredients in a saucepan and heat gently, stirring constantly until the sugar has melted. Bring the sauce to the boil and boil fast for 5 minutes, stirring occasionally to prevent sticking.

Orange and Cranberry (V)

2 blood oranges
125g (4oz) fresh or frozen cranberries
75g (3oz) golden caster sugar (unrefined)
150ml (¼ pint) water

Grate the zest away from the oranges and put to one side. Peel the oranges and segment. Put the cranberries in a small saucepan with the sugar and water. Heat gently until the sugar has dissolved, then simmer until the cranberries have softened. Drain the cranberries. Boil the liquid until syrupy, then return the cranberries to the pan with the orange slices and zest. Mix together and turn into a small bowl. Leave to cool.

Hot Blueberry (V)

2tsp cornflour
water
75g (3oz) golden caster sugar (unrefined)
zest of 1 lemon
450g (1lb) fresh or frozen blueberries

Blend the cornflour with 3 tbsp of water in a saucepan, then add another 150ml (¼ pint) water, the caster sugar, lemon zest and blueberries to the saucepan. Stir over a gentle heat until the sugar has dissolved and the mixture has thickened.

Cider (V)

This is quite fun served over a slice of a really good apple cake or, like any of the above, serve it hot over ice cream.

400ml (12fl oz) cider
1tbsp muscovado sugar
1 cinnamon stick

Put all the ingredients in a large heavy-based saucepan. Heat gently until the sugar has dissolved. Bring to the boil, then simmer until reduced by about half – this may take about 20 minutes. Remove the cinnamon stick before serving.

Raspberry (V)

450g (1lb) frozen (defrosted) or fresh raspberries
25g (1oz) golden caster sugar (unrefined)
1-2tbsp berry liqueur

Whizz the berries and sugar in a food processor until smooth and, for an ultra smooth sauce, sieve as well. Stir in the liqueur, chill and serve.